HUMANITY
Patrick Bonneville Society

THREATENED

KIM MURRAY
WITH SHANNON PARTRIDGE
AND PATRICK BONNEVILLE

HUMANITY
Patrick Bonneville Society

THREATENED

100 SPECIES ON THE VERGE OF EXTINCTION

DESIGNED BY
PATRICK BONNEVILLE

Published by
PATRICK BONNEVILLE SOCIETY
310 Parmenter, Sutton, Quebec
J0E 2K0 Canada
www.patrickbonneville.ca

Writer: Kim Murray
Research: Kim Murray, Patrick Bonneville
Editor: Shannon Partridge
Proofreading: Kelli Ann Ferrigan
Designer: Patrick Bonneville
Consultant designer: Philippe Hemono

Cover design: Patrick Bonneville
Back cover text: Shannon Partridge
Cover picture: Eric Isselée/Dreamstime.com
Half Title Page: Madd/Dreamstime.com
Full Title Page: Kitchner Bain/Dreamstime.com
Introduction: Bonfils Fabien/Dreamstime.com

Series created by Patrick Bonneville

First edition

The publisher offers special thanks to
Kim Murray, Shannon Partridge, Kelli
Ann Ferrigan, Gina Garza, Lori Baird,
Isabelle Paradis and Philippe Hemono.
The publisher also thanks Céline
Laprise, Caroline Leclerc and Louis
Dubé from the SODEC. *Merci à tous.*

Printed and bound in China

ISBN 978-1-926654-08-9

Legal deposit - Bibliothèques et Archives nation-
ales du Québec, 2010. Legal deposit - Library and
Archives Canada, 2010

Produced with the financial support of the
Government of Quebec Tax Credit for book
publishing program (SODEC) and the Sodexport
program.

This book is dedicated to Simon Stuart, Chair of IUCN's Species Survival Commission, and to everyone who participated in IUCN's Red List.

Patrick Bonneville

"We shan´t save all we should like to, but we shall save a great deal more than if we had never tried."
—Sir Peter Scott, one of the founders of WWF

Endangered Cuban crocodile

C O N T E N T S

Photo credit: Angela Campanelli

The correlation is clear: as humans grow in number, other species are rapidly shrinking. The pressure humankind puts on the world's ecosystems is leading some species straight to extinction.

We humans have the power to decide which species will and will not survive. Frankly, I don't believe that any one of us, from anywhere around the globe, wants to be responsible for the extinction of a species. Collectively, though, by focusing on the quality of our own lifestyles and livelihood, we are responsible.

The inspiration for this book is the Red List program of the International Union for the Conservation of Nature (IUCN). With its thousands of experts and scientists, the organization and its partners monitor the status of every single species on earth.

The Red List program classifies species into nine groups based on the degree of danger of extinction they face. The nine groups are:

- Extinct
- Extinct in the Wild
- Critically Endangered
- Endangered
- Vulnerable
- Near Threatened
- Least Concern
- Data Deficient
- Not Evaluated

According to IUCN Red List experts, the official term "threatened" is a grouping of three categories: critically endangered, endangered, and vulnerable. When I looked at their data, it was shocking and surprising to see how many of the species were on the verge of vanishing from our world. We couldn't launch a book series called HUMANITY without addressing this very important issue. I strongly believe than everyone should know about these threatened species.

On a more positive note, I hope this book demonstrates that we have the power to change these trends. Some of us are already working on it, creating refuges, protecting the last individuals, and educating local populations. We want to spread the word about these critical situations. Together, we can help them survive and repopulate the Earth. We can change their fates. Together, we have that power.

Patrick Bonneville

The Ranking Process

Many publishing folk and friends have asked me about the top 100 format of the HUMANITY books. Why do we choose a subjective ranking process? Well, here is my most honest answer: we want to make a statement. By listing these species in a preferential order, we can put emphasis on the ones we think are worth the most attention.

Ranking also creates debate. We want people to talk about what is happening to these species and their environments. And we want people to talk about why those things are happening. Ranking leads us to challenge and defend what is important to us and to humanity. Ranking the species challenges the way we view our lifestyle and how it impacts our environment.

On the other hand, our ranking is certainly not absolute truth. We acknowledge our Western bias. We acknowledge the limitations of our research. We also acknowledge that we are not specialists in species survival.

Some of these threatened species have to be ranked first because we deeply need them to survive. The threat of their disappearance is just too significant—for the Earth's ecosystem and, ultimately, for our own survival. For we, of course, are at the top of the food chain. Other less known species are also worth mentioning in this book; some of them are rare and rarely studied.

For the sake of space and organization, we have mostly focused on mammals, choosing to leave aside the multitudes of threatened plants, insects, reptiles, and fish.

We chose to apply five criteria in ranking these animals:

Threat
What is the level of threat according to the IUCN Red List program?

Uniqueness
Are there any related species in the world that have pretty much the same characteristics?

Human Responsibility
What is the role of humankind in the threat to the species?

Hope
Is the situation hopeless? Is it too late to change the trend?

Symbolism
Is the species an important symbol for humankind and humanity? Does it play an important role in our cultures?

Patrick Bonneville: The DNA of gorillas is 98 to 99 percent identical to that of humans. To me, the near-extinction of this species looks like genocide. Wild gorillas are stuck on the border of Rwanda and Democratic Republic of the Congo, where hard times for the human population mean hard times for the gorillas. I don't know if we are going to be able to protect them for long.

There are two types of gorilla: the western lowland species, which lives in forests, swamps, and marshes, and the mountain gorilla, which inhabits the cloud forests of higher elevations in central Africa. The lowland gorilla is evaluated as critically endangered on the IUCN Red List, and the mountain gorilla is considered endangered. The sustainability of both is threatened by the practice of poaching for bushmeat and by habitat destruction.

The mountain gorilla was discovered a mere 100 years ago; since then, humans have brought war, disease, destruction of their habitat, and capture for illegal pet trading. Their numbers have been reduced to about 700 in the wild. They are concentrated along the Virunga volcanic mountain ranges bordering the Democratic Republic of the Congo, Rwanda, Uganda, as well as in the Bwindi Impenetrable National Park in Uganda. There is debate as to whether the Bwindi and mountain gorillas belong to the same species or if they are their own unique subspecies.

Fully mature male gorillas are called silverbacks because of their light-colored backs. Males under twelve years of age are called blackbacks. Although they are born weighing about 1.8 kilograms (4 lbs), as adults they can weigh as much as 230 kilograms (about 510 lbs). Adult females are about half the size of silverbacks. Male gorillas break away from their groups just before complete maturity, alone or with peers, to eventually attract enough females to begin their own troops. Mountain gorillas are foliovores who gather and eat roots, stems, herbs, and, on occasion, insects.

In general, a mountain gorilla troop has between five and thirty members. Silverbacks are in charge of mediating conflicts, making all troop decisions, determining where and when they will move, protecting their troops, and leading them to feeding sites. A silverback remains head of his troop until he dies or is killed, or until a youth fights him out. If a troop loses its leader, members may split up in search of a new troop to join or they may respond to a younger blackback who will assume the leadership role.

Threat	10/10
Uniqueness	10/10
Human responsability	10/10
Hope	8/10
Symbolism	10/10
Average score	9.6/10

Right: Young gorillas leave their mother at the age of four at the latest.

Adult males can live to be thirty-five years old in the wild, and those kept in captivity can live as long as fifty years. Despite their capacity for aggression and manifestations of power, silverbacks show concern for the safety of their troops and even ensure that orphaned infants are cared for by the females.

Western lowland gorillas prefer lowland tropical forest habitats. In 2007, previously undocumented populations of this species were discovered in northern regions of the Republic of the Congo. Lowland gorillas are nevertheless considered the most endangered of all African gorillas. One of its subspecies, the Cross River gorilla, is on the brink of extinction, with fewer than 300 individuals left in the wild.

The western lowland species is the gorilla most often found in zoos. In the wild, they eat shoots, leaves, and fruits. Troops average ten members but are sometimes bigger, and consist of a dominant male, several females, adolescents and children, and sometimes non-dominant males.

Left: A male silverback can weigh 230 kg (510 lb).
Above: In July 2007 four gorillas were shot to death by rebels in Virunga National Park.

Western gorillas are victims of the forest industry, as their habitats are destroyed by the work of logging companies. Logging company employees also consume gorilla meat and use logging vehicles to transport bushmeat to market. The Ebola virus has caused extremely high mortality rates as well. The virus was first noted in 1994 in the Minkébé forest in northern Gabon, where there have since been three outbreaks that have affected about 600 gorillas.

Conservation efforts to save the gorilla are desperately needed. Unfortunately, war conditions in many of the gorilla's territories make it difficult for conservationists to safely do their work. Nevertheless, the Great Ape Survival Project, a UNEP/UNESCO partnership, has the objective of educating people who share the gorilla's territory about the link between their well-being and that of apes. The Agreement on the Conservation of Gorillas and their Habitats, confirmed in 2008, aims to help member states with plans to protect and conserve the gorilla. These plans include designating, protecting, and restoring habitats and synchronizing the enforcement of anti-poaching regulations.

Left: There are a few dozen gorillas in captivity in the world, mostly in zoos.
Lower left: Gorillas live in groups for protection, feeding and reproduction purposes.
Above: A dominant silverback gorilla.
Right: A few individuals in captivity have been taught a subset of sign language.

"The man who kills the animals today is the man who kills the people who get in his way tomorrow."
—Dian Fossey

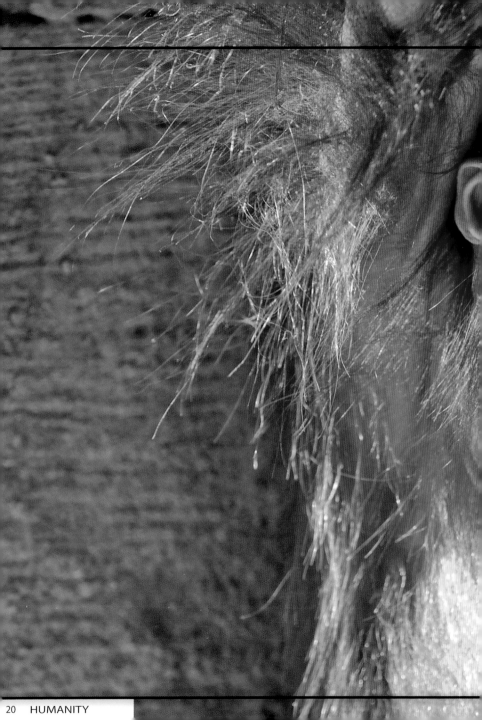

Kim Murray: We love these creatures because they are smart, comical, kind, and remind us of ourselves.

Only two species of orangutan remain on earth. Both depend on rainforests for food and shelter, and as deforestation claims their habitat, they are disappearing at a frightening rate. The Bornean orangutan is rated by the IUCN as endangered, and the Sumatran orangutan is critically endangered.

It is estimated that in the early 1900s, more than 230,000 orangutans wandered freely in Borneo and Sumatra. Today's numbers are startling: there are a mere 60,000 of them left in total, and only about 7,300 Sumatran orangutans were left on Sumatra by 2004. Since figures show that their numbers have dropped by at least 30 to 50 percent in the last ten years alone, it is logical to conclude that it will not be long before the orangutan is a species of the past.

Orangutans belong to the hominid, or great ape, family and are somewhat smaller than gorillas. They are the only great apes found in Asian regions and are the largest to live in trees. Orangutans are highly intelligent, and some groups have even been found to use tools for eating. These reddish-haired creatures can live up to fifty years and can walk upright, like humans. According to the WWF, captive orangutans released into the wild demonstrate that they can learn sophisticated skills: some have been seen untying complex nautical knots that secured boats and then using the boats to cross rivers. Even wild orangutans make tools that they use to scratch themselves or as utensils for digging, fighting, and prying things open, as when getting to the honey in a beehive.

The greatest danger facing the Sumatran orangutan is the lumber industry. Unfortunately, these tree-dwellers inhabit the northernmost tip of their island, an area covered in forests ideal for timber. Orangutans depend almost exclusively on the forests for the leaves, shoots, fruits, insects, honey, and nuts that they eat, as well as for shelter. Females virtually never touch the ground and males will do so only when necessary.

Left: Orangutans are major attractions in zoos around the world.
Upper right: Mothers and infants are very close. Orangutan mothers are often killed by poachers so the children can be sold as pets.

Another contributor to the degradation of the orangutan's habitat is the encroachment of roads and people after forests are cut down for industry. As the human population grows, so does pollution; this reduces the quality of the remaining forests and affects the diet of the orangutan. Sumatran orangutans are also illegally hunted for the international pet trade or are killed as pests when landowners catch them eating their crops or fruit. They are occasionally hunted for food.

The Bornean orangutan faces many of the same threats. In 2005, there were between 45,000 and 69,000 of them on Borneo, an island in Southeast Asia. A rapidly growing palm oil industry in Borneo equals drastic loss of natural

forest. Between 1984 and 2003, 27,000 square kilometers of land were destroyed to make way for palm farms.

Weather has also contributed to habitat loss, such as when the disastrous tsunami of 2005 caused damage and increased demand for forest products. Occasional droughts can lead to forest fires, and in some seasons, heavy rains have caused flooding. Many of these seemingly natural phenomena have been linked to global warming caused by industry. The Bornean orangutan is also a victim of illegal hunting and trading. In 2006, some fifty orangutans were confiscated from locations thousands of kilometers away from their natural dwellings and were reintroduced to the wild.

The advantages to saving the orangutan are broad: if we protect their rainforest habitat we can also contribute to the endurance of other species, such as the proboscis monkey, the Asian elephant, the Sumatran rhinoceros, the Sumatran tiger, the clouded leopard, the Malayan sun bear, and the Malay tapirs. In 2007, Indonesian President Soesilo Bambang Yudhoyono initiated the Orangutan Conservation Strategy and Action Plan, which is designed to protect the animal and ensure its habitat does not suffer from climate change.

There are further advantages to conservation, ones that extend to us humans: if we protect rainforests, which filter our air and offset carbon emissions, then we save the air we ourselves breathe.

"Our nightmares are becoming government policy and coming very close to home. Indonesia has just entered the Guinness Book of World Records as having the fastest rate of deforestation in the world."
—Dr. Biruté Mary Galdikas, founder of the Orangutan Foundation International (OFI).

Left: An orangutan can live over 60 years in captivity and in the wild as well.
Above: A baby orangutan holds on to its mother.
Right: Orangutans spend most of their days searching for and consuming food.

"The survival of orangutans and other rainforest wildlife in Indonesia is seriously endangered by illegal logging, forest fires, including those associated with the rapid spread of oil palm plantations, illegal hunting and trade."
—UNEP

Threat	9.5/10
Uniqueness	10/10
Human responsability	10/10
Hope	8/10
Symbolism	9/10
Average score	9.3/10

Kim Murray: Once upon a time it was believed that the giant panda was part of the raccoon family; it is easy to see why, with its black and white coat and dark eye patches.

This bear's scientific name is *Ailuropoda melanoleuca*, which literally means "cat-foot black-and-white." These endangered pandas are native to China's Yangtze River basin, where the IUCN believes that there are fewer than 2,500 individuals left in the wild, with no more than 250 in any one population group.

Although the panda is part of the order *Carnivora*, it almost exclusively eats bamboo. When pandas can, they supplement their diet with fish, eggs, bananas, and a few other foods. They spend just over half their time feeding, during the day and night. The reproductive habits of the wild panda are similar to those of other bears: females may give birth to one or two cubs, although she will only care for one of them. Adults are solitary, except during breeding times and during the raising of a young bear.

"The giant panda is one of these species threatened to be wiped off the planet. Ironically, it is also one of the better known and loved species in the world and one of the strongest symbols of nature conservation."
—WWF

The bear's natural range is in the geographic and economic heart of China; millions of people inhabit this part of the Sichuan province, and so habitat degradation seems inevitable. In the past, bear groups would move to new forests when their source of bamboo trees naturally died off. Today, however, there are fewer places for the bear to move, and they are forced to eat less nutritious species of bamboo. During past decades, pandas were also given as gifts and were hunted for their fur. Today, poachers receive severe punishment and the sale of panda pelts has all but disappeared.

Conservation efforts are on the rise to make the region sustainable for this and other endangered species—such as the dwarf blue sheep, the golden monkey, and the crested ibis—that share its habitat. The Chinese government has established panda reserves, although even some of these are compromised by human intrusion. Luckily, the giant panda plays an important symbolic role in Chinese culture, which is as good a motivation for conservation as any.

Threat	8.5/10
Uniqueness	10/10
Human responsability	9.5/10
Hope	8.5/10
Symbolism	10/10
Average score	9.3/10

Right: Giant panda in its protected natural habitat, province of Sichuan, Central China.

This rare native to western African forests and swamps is one of only two extant species in the Hippopotamidae family; the other is its much larger cousin, the common hippopotamus. It is estimated that there are fewer than 3,000 pygmy hippos in the wild, and this figure is expected to decline by 20 percent over the next twenty years. They are threatened by a variety of factors, most notably habitat loss, poaching, hunting, natural predators, and war. The IUCN Red List ranks the pygmy hippo as endangered.

Endemic to Sierra Leone, Republic of Guinea, Côte d'Ivoire, and Liberia, these nocturnal animals are difficult to study in the wild. Most of what is known about pygmy hippos comes from captive animals in zoos, where they are successfully bred. They are solitary and semi-aquatic: they rely on immersion in water to keep their skin moist and to regulate their body temperature, however they spend time on land as well. These herbivores eat ferns, broad-leaf plants, grasses, and fruits.

Although their habitat had already been dwindling for more than a century, the explosion in human development over last thirty years has brought great change to the pygmy hippo. Their historical ranges have been logged, farmed, and settled. Forced into deeper forests, population groups have become segregated. Armed conflict in many African countries has placed added pressure on the hippo, and war zones are frequently considered too dangerous for conservationists to do their work.

Despite official protected status in Guinea, Côte d'Ivoire, and Sierra Leone, there do not appear to be any real enforcement measures in place. Reports suggest that resources are lacking. In Liberia, where most pygmy hippos reside, the IUCN deems conservation efforts as incomplete in the face of massive deforestation.

It appears that the only hope for the present is captive breeding. The number of captive-born pygmy hippos has more than doubled since 1970. Nevertheless, it is generally agreed that zoo animals are physically and psychologically stressed by their captivity, and, obviously, such measures do little to improve conditions for the species in the wild.

Left: Pygmy hippos spend most of their time hiding and resting in rivers.
Above: Pygmy hippos are herbivorous.

Threat	10/10
Uniqueness	9/10
Human responsability	10/10
Hope	10/10
Symbolism	7/10
Average score	9.2/10

Threat	10/10
Uniqueness	9/10
Human responsability	10/10
Hope	10/10
Symbolism	7/10
Average score	9.2/10

Patrick Bonneville: Scientists agree: the vaquita is likely the next species to vanish completely from the waters of the Earth. It is just a matter of time.

The vaquita is a rare species of porpoise whose Spanish name means "little cow." It lives in the Sea of Cortez along the northern part of the Gulf of California. The use of gillnets in commercial fishing has led to a drastic drop in population numbers; it is estimated that there are as few as one to three hundred individuals left.

Although vaquitas resemble common porpoises, they are stockier and have a rounder face. They are also the smallest of porpoises, weighing up to fifty kilograms (110.2 lbs). These mammals breathe air and prefer to skim the surface of the water and disappear for long periods between breaths.

Experts agree that the main reason for its near-disappearance is accidental trapping in fishing gillnets. The Committee for the Recovery of the Vaquita estimates that between thirty-nine and eighty porpoises are killed each year in this way. A second negative effect of gillnet and trawl net fishing is that the vaquita's food sources are often also caught as bycatch; this means a reduced food supply.

Another threat comes from hydroelectric damming, which causes habitat damage. The damming of the Colorado River in the U.S.A. has had especially deleterious effects on the vaquita, as it reduces the input of freshwater to the vaquita's environment. Natural predators are reducing the already vulnerable porpoise population. In ordinary circumstances predators would have little impact on the long-term sustainability of a population; however, since the number of vaquitas remaining in the wild is so low, experts feel the need to address the issue. Projects to deter the white shark, mako, and other fish species from feeding on vaquitas are in the works.

The WWF in Mexico and the United States are working on a long-term strategy for restoring numbers and preserving the species. Their conservation program outlines a goal to reduce the number of vaquitas caught as bycatch to no more than one per year. Measures proposed to achieve this include the establishment of reserves where gillnet and shrimp trawls are forbidden.

Many of those who live along the shores of the vaquita's habitat practice the kind of fishing that endangers the porpoise, and care must be taken to ensure that other programs are in place to support the economic needs of local communities. Sustainable development measures are necessary in order to protect both the vaquita and the fishermen who depend on the ocean for their livelihoods.

Opposite page: Vaquitas live in the Sea of Cortez. **Left:** Vaquita stuck in fishing nets.

Patrick Bonneville: It is a spectacular sight to watch this giant black bird fly over the Grand Canyon.

This vulture is one of the longest-living birds in the world, with a lifespan of up to fifty years. Poaching, lead poisoning, and habitat destruction all but wiped this species off the face of the earth, and in 1987, there were only twenty-two birds left. The IUCN ranks the California condor as critically endangered.

It is the largest North American land bird and is now found only in the Grand Canyon region, Zion National Park, and from the western coastal mountains of California south to northern Baja California. In 1987, the American government captured all remaining wild birds and began a breeding program at the San Diego Wild Animal Park and the Los Angeles Zoo. By 1991, the population was strong enough to reintroduce individuals to the wild. In April 2009, there were some 300 known condors alive, including 170 in the wild. This program was the most expensive species conservation endeavor ever undertaken by the United States.

Several threats remain for the California condor in the wild, especially from shooting and lead poisoning. When these scavengers feed upon carcasses left behind by hunters, they also ingest the lead-based bullets used as ammunition. With continuous consumption of lead over a bird's long lifespan, the metal builds up to toxic levels and causes an unnatural death. The American government has taken measures to ban the use of lead ammunition in the condor's territory. They have also introduced education programs that are intended to raise public awareness about the problem. Public education also focuses on decreasing pollution, as two nestlings were recently found with glass fragments, wire, and plastic in their stomachs.

A further challenge for the bird is a by-product of the breeding program. Condors that are bred in captivity show no fear of humans; when placed in the wild they boldly approach human settlements, where they ingest garbage pollution and are vulnerable to accidental killing based on fear. Birds raised by adult condors, however, learn to avoid humans.

"In 1985, the wild population of California condors consisted of nine individuals."
—The California Condor Recovery Program

Upper left: Few California condors can be seen in the Grand Canyon National Park.
Right: Most California condors are marked and can be monitored.

Threat	9.5/10
Uniqueness	9/10
Human responsability	10/10
Hope	8/10
Symbolism	9/10
Average score	9.1/10

Patrick Bonneville: Let's hope this flightless bird, the pride of New Zealand and one of its national symbols, will be with us forever.

New Zealand has four species of kiwi birds; three of them are vulnerable or near-endangered, and one of them, the North Island brown kiwi, is considered endangered by the IUCN. Although numbers are stabilizing through conservation efforts, and all the sub-species together form a total population of 35,000, an alarming 94 percent of chicks die before they reach breeding age.

About the size of a chicken, the kiwi evolved as a flightless bird due to the lack of land predators in its natural habitat. Males and females tend to mate for life, which is about twenty years. Traditionally, the kiwi was believed to be under the protection of the Maori god of the forest, Tane Mahuta. The Maori, who once hunted the bird but who now venerate it, decorate their ceremonial cloaks with kiwi feathers collected from dead birds or gathered in the forests. The word "kiwi" was given to New Zealand soldiers during World War I and is now a common nickname designating all New Zealanders.

The most common of the species, the North Island brown kiwi, has the healthiest population base, at around 25,000. It is found throughout the northern region of the North Island. The majority of chicks are killed by predators, especially non-native cats, dogs, and other small mammals. Smaller populations throughout the islands are threatened with habitat loss.

Education and conservation efforts on the part of New Zealand involve strict monitoring systems including radio-tracking, trained dog searches, and call-counts. Organizations are in place with personnel to collect eggs and place them in incubators before they can be attacked by predators; once birds are old enough to fend for themselves, they are released into the wild. With sustained territory protection and predator control, it is hoped kiwi numbers will stabilize indefinitely.

"The kiwi is a biological oddity and full of character. More than any other native animal, they are entwined in our identity as New Zealanders."
—*The BNZ Save the Kiwi Trust*

Threat	9/10
Uniqueness	9.5/10
Human responsability	8/10
Hope	8/10
Symbolism	10/10
Average score	8.9/10

Right: Monitoring kiwis in the wild.

Patrick Bonneville: This gracious blue parrot means big business for some people—it has a market value of up to $10,000. Owners of these pets should feed them well, because soon there will no longer be any to buy.

The hyacinth macaw is the largest flying parrot in the world. Once prevalent throughout Central and South America, it is now almost exclusively found in Pantanal, a state in central Brazil bordering Paraguay and Bolivia. The IUCN considers it endangered, since there are estimated to be fewer than 6,500 left in the wild.

These macaws can have a wingspan of up to 120-140 cm (56 inches). In their natural habitat, they nest in holes in trees where a single fledgling will survive the struggle with its siblings for food. Young birds stay with their parents until three months of age. Adults have no known predators, although eggs and young macaws are eaten by other species.

Because of their striking appearance, hyacinth macaws are coveted as pets. Thousands of them were trapped throughout the 1980s, mostly for Brazilian pet owners. This illegal trade continues today, although it is not as common. There is also some traditional hunting by local tribes who kill the macaw for food and for feathers used in cultural artifacts. Habitat loss from cattle-ranching and hydro-electric projects are also threats.

The Brazilian and Bolivian governments have placed the bird under protection by law and have banned all exports of the macaw. Education programs are in place to ensure that cattle farmers understand the importance of this species. The Hyacinth Macaw Project has also used artificial nests and chick management programs to ensure survival.

"The purpose of my work, which means my life, is to preserve the hyacinth macaw in the wild. I don't care about having 100, 200, or 300 birds in captivity 50 or 100 years from now. I care about a sustainable population of hyacinth macaws flying free in Brazil." —Biologist Neiva Guedes, founder of the Hyacinth Macaw Project, started in 1990

Threat	9/10
Uniqueness	9.5/10
Human responsability	9/10
Hope	9/10
Symbolism	7.5/10
Average score	8.8/10

Right: This giant parrot's distinctive coloring makes it one of the most unique birds in the world.

Patrick Bonneville: Whales are the biggest animals on earth. And yet they are so graceful and non-threatening to humans. Whale oil fed the industrial revolution and whales have been featured in human stories for centuries: they even appear in the Bible and in the Qur'an. If any of their species disappear from our oceans, we are the only ones to blame.

There are many species of whales, some more at risk of extinction than others. Humans have hunted many of the species for centuries, and our actions have led to the near extinction of many of them. The sei whale, blue whale, fin whale, and the North Atlantic and North Pacific right whales are five species that appear on the IUCN Red List as endangered. Some of their sub-populations are critically endangered. All five species have experienced population declines of about 70 to 90 percent in the last ninety years.

Previously endangered species, such as the humpback and Southern right whale, have been downlisted to vulnerable, thanks to bans on commercial harvesting.

Commerical fishing is the main cause for the abysmal decline in whale populations. Much of the United States' rise in the ninetheenth century as an industrial nation was literally fueled by whale oil. It greased textile and manufacturing machines and was used in candles to light homes. Vast quantities of whalebone were used in corsets to uphold the fashions of the time. The replacement of whale oil with mineral oil came rather too late: whale populations were already drastically depleted.

Early fishing bans introduced in the first half of the twentieth century were often poorly enforced, leaving some species populations to dwindle to fewer than one hundred adult individuals. Some countries, such as the former USSR, Spain, and Japan persisted in the fishery until zero tolerance laws began to be enforced for most species in the late 1970s and 1980s.

Left: Whaling vessels in Reykjavík harbour, Iceland. The country resumed commercial whaling in 2006 despite international protest.
Upper right: Excessive whaling through the ages has lead to the current critical situation.
Lower right: Whaling in the Faroe Islands, located between the UK and Iceland.

The hunt for blue, fin, and sei whales began after other easier-to-catch species were nearly fished out and modern whaling techniques were developed. The right whale has been continuously fished for over 150 years. In the period between 1840 and 1849, about 30,000 were hunted. As late as 1909, it was estimated that the population of the North Pacific right whale hovered between 26,500 and 37,000; since 2000, however, only three North Pacific right whales have been seen. During the twentieth century, not a single right whale calf has been observed.

The eastern North Atlantic sub-population is currently estimated at fewer than fifty mature individuals. Except

for special permission for infrequent aboriginal whale hunts, hunting of the right whale in the North Atlantic ended by 1990. Both Iceland and Japan have been granted permission to return to fin whale hunting, although their yearly catches are small, due, in part, to a reduced market demand.

Although hunting is banned, right whales are frequently victims of shipping accidents and accidents with fishing gear. Based on observation of scarring, it is estimated that about 72 percent of the right whale population has undergone net entanglement at some point. Current studies also indicate that poor nutrition, chemical contaminants, biotoxins, and disease contribute to the low population of right whales.

The United States and Canada have both tabled programs to further protect the right whale from accidents due to the shipping and fishing industries. The USA has tabled regulations that would require modifications to fishing gear and restrictions on the use of certain equipment in right whale territories. As well, shipping lanes through the Bay of Fundy are moved during the summer months to accommodate for the return migration of the right whale.

"Humpbacks and southern right whales are making a comeback in much of their range mainly because they have been protected from commercial hunting. This is a great conservation success and clearly shows what needs to be done to ensure these ocean giants survive."
—*Randall Reeves, Chair of the Cetacean Specialist Group of the IUCNSpecies Survival Commission*

Threat	8/10
Uniqueness	9/10
Human responsability	10/10
Hope	7/10
Symbolism	10/10
Average score	8.8/10

Below: A young girl watching a fisherman cut a small whale into pieces.
Right: Whale watching from the beach at sunset.

Patrick Bonneville: This big cat, Panthera tigris, is spectacular. One of the greatest carnivores of the world, it has fed our imaginations for centuries. It does not deserve to be held captive in zoos or even worse, in circuses or in Las Vegas. It deserves the kind of safe haven like they have in India's Project Tiger.

Tigers are the largest of the big cats in the Felidae family and can still be found throughout eastern and southern Asia. With a total wild population of only about 3,400 to 5,000 adults, the tiger is listed as endangered on the IUCN Red List. Three of the nine subspecies of the modern tiger are now extinct. The remaining six are endangered, and some are listed as critically endangered. Clearly, this species has the bad luck of being in the path of human beings.

"The tiger, largest of all cats, is one of the most charismatic and evocative species on Earth; it is also one of the most threatened."
—WWF

Historically, the tiger roamed freely from Turkey in the west to Siberia in the north and as far as the eastern coast of Asia. Today, they have lost an incredible 93 percent of their historic range and can only be sparsely found in twelve Asian states. These solitary creatures can weigh as much as 300 kilograms (660 lbs). The tiger is an apex predator, meaning it is not preyed upon by any other animal—except by humans. The most numerous subspecies is the Bengal tiger, while the largest in stature is the Siberian tiger.

The most current threat to the tiger is human population growth. Since the human population has exploded in Asia and continues to grow, the conversion of forest space for human settlement is widespread. Tigers feed on deer and wild pigs, and when these food sources disappear, so do tigers. While there are cases of attacks on humans, in general, tigers do not enter villages unless they are starving. It is common practice in most areas to kill a tiger if it enters a village or if a human has been attacked. Tigers were once victims of extensive poaching, however there is an international ban on hunting the cats today. And although CITES protects them through its international trade ban on tiger products, the rather unethical practice of tiger farming continues.

Left: Cub in Indian tiger reserves. Project Tiger, a wildlife conservation movement, was initiated in India in 1972 to protect Bengal tigers.
Right: According to a poll conducted by Animal Planet, the tiger was voted the world's favourite animal, ahead of dogs and horses.

Shockingly, there are more tigers kept as pets in the United States than there are in the wild. According to the Association of Zoos and Aquariums, about 12,000 tigers are kept as private pets; there are an incredible 4,000 in Texas alone. Nineteen states ban private ownership of tigers, fifteen states require a license, and sixteen have no regulations at all.

Tigers have a low recruitment rate. This means few adults raise young that survive and join breeding populations. They also have low density rates, meaning they require large ranges in order to survive. Current protected zones in Bangladesh, Bhutan, Cambodia, China, India, Indonesia, Lao PDR, Malaysia, Myanmar, Nepal, Russia, Thailand, and Viet Nam are simply too small to accommodate the tiger's range.

Fortunately, humans also want to keep the tiger in existence. More than forty National Tiger Conservation Authority (Project Tiger) wildlife reserves cover some 37.75 km^2 in India. These reserves helped to boost the declining population of tigers from a precarious 1,200 in the 1970s to 3,500 in the 1990s. In 2008, however, following a census by the government of India, the tiger population was once again under the 1,500 mark. Consequently, a Tiger Protection Force was initiated at a cost of $US 153 million. The force will tackle poachers and relocate about 200,000 villagers in an effort to reduce interaction with the wild animals.

Left: Tigers are still used in circuses.
Upper right: Many tigers are kept as domestic pets.

Education is essential for any long-term projects to conserve the wild tiger. For the overall well-being of the species, it is particularly important that illegal trade in consumer products from tiger farms be curbed through education and better policing.

"The striking white coat is caused by a double recessive allele in the genetic code, and only turns up naturally about once in every 10,000 births. Amazingly, the Bengal tiger is the only subspecies in which it seems to happen. As beautiful as it may look, life as a white tiger can't be easy when your life depends on being able to hide from and/or sneak up on things."
—Indian Tiger Welfare Society

Threat	8/10
Uniqueness	9/10
Human responsability	10/10
Hope	7/10
Symbolism	10/10
Average score	8.8/10

"(The)tiger is a symbol of wilderness and well-being of the ecosystem. By conserving and saving tigers the entire wilderness ecosystem is conserved. In nature, barring human beings and their domesticates, the rest of the ecosystem is wild. Hence conserving wilderness is important and crucial to maintain the life support system. So saving the tiger amounts to saving the ecosystem which is crucial for man's own survival."
—*Project Tiger, sponsored by the Government of India*

11 - TUNA

Patrick Bonneville: No more tuna fish sandwiches! Tuna is being fished at too fast a rate. On top of that, this fishing industry also kills many other species as collateral damage.

There are twenty-three identified species of tuna, most of which have been completely or nearly fished to endangerment and extinction. At least nine species of tuna are classified as fully fished out, and another four are overexploited or depleted. Three are listed as critically endangered, including the southern bluefin tuna, another three are classed as endangered, and three more are considered vulnerable to extinction. It is clearly time for humans to begin caring for our oceans and their inhabitants.

The world's fishing industry has the capacity to catch greater quantities of tuna than is legally allowed. In 2002, some tuna species were fished at 70 percent over quotas. The catch is used for canned tuna and for Japan's sushi market. Overfishing imposes serious concerns not just for tuna stocks but also for the thousands of pounds of by-catch, such as dolphins, whales, turtles, and even seabirds, that are caught in tuna nets.

Although some conservation and management programs are in place, protection of this species today is inadequate. It is essential that the fishing quotas be monitored and the industry policed in order to halt the disappearance of the tuna.

"We now have too much experience to ignore on how fast overexploited fisheries collapse and how slowly, if at all, they recover. With Bluefin tuna none of the collapsed populations are recovering and the remaining populations are clearly heading towards collapse."
—Miguel Jorge, Marine Director at WWF International

Above: Freshly fished tuna, one of the most important commercial fish in the world.
Right: Our appetite for tuna is leading the species to extinction.

Threat	8/10
Uniqueness	9/10
Human responsability	10/10
Hope	9.5/10
Symbolism	7/10
Average score	8.7/10

The Sumatran rhinoceros is the smallest of the five existing rhino species. Once common to ancient rainforests throughout the Indian subcontinent, Southeast Asia, and China, today they are found in Sumatra, Borneo, and Malaysia. About 300 individuals are alive in the wild, leading the IUCN Red List to rank them as critically endangered.

Also called the hairy rhino because of its reddish-brown coat of hair, this animal is solitary except for when breeding and raising young, which occurs once every three years. The largest populations live in the thick tropical forests of three national parks on Indonesia's island of Sumatra. They are opportunistic feeders who forage a wide variety of plant life. The Sumatran rhino can live as long as forty years.

Poaching is the main cause of the Sumatran rhino's disappearance from the wild. A traditional ingredient in Chinese medicine, Sumatran rhino horn is worth as much as $30,000 on the black market. Habitat loss is also a factor, as logging and the transformation of forest into agricultural land increases. Because rhino populations are scattered, breeding and reproduction are difficult to accomplish.

The species was placed on the CITES Appendix I in 1975 and is legally protected in all range states. Whereas an earlier captive conservation project was unsuccessful, an international effort is being implemented in Indonesia and Malaysia to ensure the sustainability of the Sumatran rhino. The primary objective is to end poaching so that populations can reach self-sufficiency. Rhino Protection Units are seen as a great aid in stopping poaching in Sumatra, and the expansion and reinforcement of these programs is top priority.

Captive breeding programs involving more than twenty animals in Indonesia, Malaysia, and the United States have also shown small successes. Successful births at the Cincinnati Zoo in 2001 and again in 2004 are proof that there is hope—one of these young rhinos was returned to Sumatra to be introduced to the wild.

"The smallest of the rhino species, the Sumatran Rhino now faces extinction. The use of its horns and other body parts in traditional Chinese medicine creates a demand that greedy poachers are eager to fill."
—Asia Geographic

Right: A captive breeding program for the Sumatran rhinoceros exists, but it hasn't been as succesful as expected. A controversial program, it is expensive and has not proven effective for the species' survival.

Threat	10/10
Uniqueness	8/10
Human responsability	9.5/10
Hope	9/10
Symbolism	7/10
Average score	8.7/10

Traditionally found in central and eastern Europe, the Iberian lynx is related to the Eurasian lynx, Canada lynx, and North American bobcat. Found today in small pockets of southwestern Spain, it is unknown if there are any individuals remaining in Portugal. With an adult population estimated to be between 84 and 143 cats, the Iberian lynx is listed as critically endangered on the IUCN Red List.

Its lack of adaptability makes the Iberian lynx a naturally vulnerable wild animal. It preys on one species only—the rabbit, which is itself habitat-specific—and is endangered by human encroachment. Increases in vehicle traffic are the cause of many deaths. It is believed that car collisions with lynx caused the cat population to dwindle by 80 percent between 1960 and 1990. The lynx is also vulnerable to illegal hunting and snares set to trap other creatures. A relatively new threat is the proposed construction of dams. The Spanish National Hydrological Plan is designing twelve dams that will directly impact the survival of this species.

To preserve the Iberian lynx, extreme conservation efforts combined with increased breeding programs must be adopted in the short term. In the long term, it is vital that priority be given to maintaining a healthy habitat rich in rabbits, with strict supervision and protection. The Spanish government has moved to establish protective regions, and a total of seventy-four sites have been proposed. These would provide more than 2.7 million hectares of land as protected areas.

The WWF and SOS Lynx agree that if the cat were to become extinct, it would be the first big cat species to succumb to such a fate in 10,000 years.

"Spain and EU fail world's most endangered cat species."
—WWF, March 2005

Threat	9/10
Uniqueness	7.5/10
Human responsability	9.5/10
Hope	8.5/10
Symbolism	9/10
Average score	8.7/10

Opposite page: Two of the last Iberian lynx, on the verge of extinction.
Left: Iberian lynx in captivity.

The jaguar is one of the big cats and is the only Panthera species found in the Americas. It is the third-largest wild cat after the tiger and the lion. Currently, the IUCN Red List describes the jaguar as near-threatened, however loss of habitat, poaching of the jaguar and its prey, and fragmentation of groups mean an inevitable relisting of the jaguar as a vulnerable species.

This powerful cat gets its name from the Native American word *yaguar,* which means "he who kills with one leap." It looks similar to a leopard, although bigger, and behaves like a tiger: it can climb, crawl, and swim. This solitary predator is not too picky about its prey, as its powerful bite allows it to hunt animals much bigger than itself. Jaguars' jaws are strong enough to destroy the shells of armored reptiles and bite through the skulls of their prey.

The jaguar is the fiercest wild cat in the Western Hemisphere. It is found in Mexico, Paraguay, and parts of northern Argentina. In the United States, there are reports of breeding populations in Arizona, New Mexico, and possibly Texas, although the jaguar has not been officially documented in the USA since the early 1900s. It is a national symbol of Brazil and has always had a special place in Brazilian culture. Native tribes believed that jaguar fat gave them courage, and it was rubbed onto the bodies of boys to protect them against evil and make them stronger.

Right: The jaguar appears on Brazilian currency.
Opposite page: The muscled feline weighs around 56–96 kilograms (124–211 lbs).

The jaguar prefers dense rainforests and tree cover. Widespread deforestation throughout Central and South American countries means the cat is vulnerable to population decline. Ranchers and farmers kill jaguars as pests since they are known to attack and kill cattle. CITES is aggressive in its control of pelt trading, although the high demand for jaguar paws, teeth, and other by-products leads to poaching.

The jaguar is fully protected at the national level across most of its range, with hunting prohibited in Argentina, Brazil, Colombia, French Guiana, Honduras, Nicaragua, Panama, Paraguay, Suriname, United States, and Venezuela. In accordance with CITES Appendix I, hunting restrictions are in place in Brazil, Costa Rica, Guatemala, Mexico, and Peru.

Threat	8/10
Uniqueness	8/10
Human responsability	8.5/10
Hope	8.5/10
Symbolism	10/10
Average score	8.6/10

Threat	7/10
Uniqueness	10/10
Human responsability	10/10
Hope	6/10
Symbolism	10/10
Average score	8.6/10

Grévy's zebra, sometimes known as the imperial zebra, is found in Kenya and Ethiopia. It is considered endangered, since its population has declined by an alarming 50 percent in twenty years.

Total numbers are low, with an estimated 750 mature animals in the wild today.

The largest of all wild horses, Grévy's zebra is distinguished from other zebras by its large ears and narrow stripes. They are heavy eaters, mostly of grasses, and can spend the bulk of the day grazing. The name comes from its role as a precious gift to French president Jules Grévy in the 1880s, when he received one from the government of Abyssinia, the former Ethiopian empire.

This zebra has experienced the most significant population decline of any African mammal. Confined to the Horn of Africa, they are in direct competition for food and water with domestic livestock and are vulnerable to disease. Their grazing grounds have been considerably reduced and they are sometimes seen as a threat by herders and farmers. Populations of Grévy's zebra in different regions are affected by different circumstances: hunting is widespread in Ethiopia, although it has seen a drop in the more stable Kenya. All zebras have fallen victim to hunters for their skins and meat.

While Grevy's zebra is legally protected in Ethiopia, there seems to be little official protection: management is inadequate, and the species remains vulnerable to illegal hunting. Kenya is currently in the process of bestowing legally protected status on this zebra. There is some good news: including young members of the population, there could be as many as 2,447 Grévy's zebras, and these numbers appear to be stable.

Conservation efforts throughout Grévy's zebra territories must focus on protection of water supplies, management of protected areas, community conservation, education, and monitoring of wild populations.

"The arid homes of many equids are also home to human populations that face the same extreme environmental pressures."
—*Dr Patricia Moehlman, IUCN*

Left: Close-up of a Grévy's zebra eye.
Right: A young Grevy's Zebra scratching its neck against a dead tree branch.

The black rhinoceros is native to eastern and central Africa, where there are just over 4,000 in the wild. The IUCN lists three subspecies as critically endangered, while a fourth West-African subspecies is probably extinct.

The black rhino is not black, its skin is of a grayish brown tone with sometimes a white hue. Its name was given to distinguish this species from its cousin, the white rhinoceros—another misnomer, from the Dutch word *wijd,* referring to the animal's wide upper lip.

As late as the last century, several hundred thousand black rhinos were scattered across eastern and southern Africa. By the 1990s, European settlers had decimated the population through widespread poaching in pursuit of the valuable rhino horn. Rhino horn is comprised of tightly compressed hair-like fibers, which many people believe to hold medicinal properties, while others use horn for decorative knife-handles and the like. Between 1970 and 1992, the illegal harvesting of horns caused a 96 percent drop in black rhino numbers.

Unfortunately, rhinos still remain an easy target, as their horns can be cut off and easily concealed for smuggling. This lucrative trade is tempting for poverty-stricken local peoples. Policing for contraband and protecting the black rhino in the wild requires extensive manpower and is extremely costly.

The World Wildlife Fund has been actively protecting the black rhino for forty years; thanks to conservation efforts, the population is slowly increasing. While some regions of Africa no longer have any species, others are seeing a slight improvement in numbers. To help ensure a continued upward trend in the population, all trade in black rhinos and their products is banned internationally. There are also efforts to concentrate the animals in fenced sanctuaries and conservancies where personnel can track and guard them.

"One of the greatest challenges facing the future of rhinos in Africa is maintaining sufficient conservation expenditure and field effort. Illegal demand for horn, high unemployment, poverty, demand for land, wars, the ready availability of arms and internal instability also pose a threat to rhino populations."
—Dr Taye Teferi, WWF's African Rhino Coordinator

Left: Black rhinoceros resting in captivity.
Right: A mother and its offspring enjoying the African western wilderness.

Threat	10/10
Uniqueness	8/10
Human responsability	9.5/10
Hope	7.5/10
Symbolism	8/10
Average score	8.6/10

Threat	10/10
Uniqueness	9/10
Human responsability	9/10
Hope	9/10
Symbolism	6/10
Average score	8.6/10

Patrick Bonneville: This animal is a very fast runner, and its drop in population was fast too. Within a decade or two, this species fell from one million individuals to a paltry 40,000.

Saiga tatarica is an ancient antelope species that once roamed the great regions of the Eurasian Steppe zone, from Hungary in the west to the far eastern regions of Mongolia. The IUCN lists the saiga as critically endangered, and the WWF treats the saiga as a priority species, meaning they consider it to be an ecologically or economically important species on our planet.

The odd-looking saiga is easily recognized by its oversized, flexible trunk-like nose that is used to filter out the dust that blows across the plains it inhabits. Today, this nomadic herd animal can be found in only a few remaining regions of Russia's Kalmykia, Kazakhstan, and western Mongolia, where it roams freely across borders in search of grazing areas.

In the early 1990s, there were more than one million saiga in the wild; some twenty years later, estimates put the total at around 40,000. Over 90 percent of males can die of exhaustion in the rutting season. These special creatures are hunted for their fur, meat, and horns, which are used in traditional Chinese medicine.

Left: The saiga has an unusual and over-sized nose structure.
Right: The species will eat anything that looks like grass, including poisonous herbs.

Despite initiatives in the 1930s and again in the 1990s to create protected areas, the saiga is clearly in danger. Further efforts by the Russian federal government will be helpful in developing protected zones where migration can take place safely and where edible grasses can be ensured for the saiga. Despite promising reproductive rates that give rise to hope that the population can rebound, further efforts to curb the saiga hunt must also be made. Uncontrolled illegal hunting, especially for horns, is still rampant. To combat this demand, experts have suggested a total and complete ban on all hunting and on the trade of all saiga meat and horn products.

"Saiga antelopes are one of the world's most rapidly declining species, their numbers falling by 95 % in just 15 years."
—The Saiga Conservation Alliance

Along with gorillas, chimpanzees are our closest cousins in the animal kingdom. They belong to the same family as humans: the Hominidae family, or the "great apes." Listed as endangered by the IUCN, chimpanzees were once found in twenty-five African countries but are now extinct in at least three. In 2003, estimates put the total population at just under 300,000. Chimp populations in many of the countries are near extinction.

The common chimpanzee lives in West and Central Africa, and the bonobo chimpanzee lives in the Democratic Republic of the Congo. They move about on the ground, but nest in trees to sleep safely. While they typically walk using both hands and feet, chimpanzees are able to walk upright as far as one kilometer. Humans often feel an attachment to chimpanzees, presumably because they remind us of ourselves as they groom each other, play, and cradle their young.

The bushmeat trade, or the selling of chimpanzee and other kinds of wild meat, poses a serious threat to forest biodiversity in several regions of Africa. Paradoxically, the market for bushmeat is exacerbated by the gap between rich and poor; no longer simply a source of food for subsistence-living residents of these areas, bushmeat is now sold by them for premium prices at urban markets where it is considered a delicacy. Often the infant of a slaughtered mother will be captured and sold as a pet to wealthy citizens or foreigners.

A further menace to the chimp is disease. Ebola has had a devastating impact on chimpanzee numbers in the northern regions of the Republic of Congo, where it is responsible for a drastic decrease in population. As with so many other species, the ultimate threat to chimpanzees is habitat degradation. As logging, slash and burn farming, and mineral and oil exploitation destroy the forests it lives in, the chimp is limited to smaller areas and is increasingly exposed to poaching.

The WWF is working on conservation efforts with local governments. Increased enforcement of protection laws, dialogue with industry, and education about the trade of illegal bushmeat are essential initiatives.

Above: Relaxing on a branch in the Congolese forest.
Right: A young bonobo posing for the camera.

Threat	8/10
Uniqueness	10/10
Human responsability	8/10
Hope	7/10
Symbolism	10/10
Average score	8.6/10

Threat	10/10
Uniqueness	8/10
Human responsability	10/10
Hope	10/10
Symbolism	4/10
Average score	8.4/10

Patrick Bonneville: I thought dolphins only lived in the sea. Then, one day, I read that river dolphins in China were extinct. I was shocked; a mammal species had just become extinct and I had not even known it existed. That was when I realized I had to learn more about all threatened species.

Six species of dolphin live in fresh-water rivers or salt-water estuaries. The baiji, also known as the Yangtze River dolphin, was declared "functionally extinct" on December 13, 2006. The last sighting of this species dates back to 2004. Several others are listed as vulnerable or endangered. Overfishing, hydroelectric damming, and sonar pollution are strongly suspected as the causes of its demise.

River dolphins are found in some of the world's greatest rivers: the Ganges, the Indus, the Yangtze, the Mekong, the Orinoco, and the Amazon. Since humans also dwell along these major rivers, conflict seems inevitable. Clearly, the effects of the fishing and shipping industries are not reserved for ocean dwelling creatures. Pollution has degraded the natural environment of all river dolphins. The stomach contents of nearly half of all dolphins examined from Brazil's Rio Grande do Sul revealed fishing gear, nylon nets, cellophane, and plastics. Demands for hydro-energy in other areas have resulted in drastic alterations of river ecosystems.

River dolphin species are in drastic need of protection. Immediate action to preserve their habitat must be taken.

Left: Baby pink dolphin at zoo near Iquitos, Peru.
Upper right: Two young river dolphins in the Amazon.
Above: The Amazon common river dolphin is also commonly known as the boto.

"Regarded in China as the "goddess of the Yangtze," the 20 million-year-old river dolphin was one of the world's oldest species. The Baiji is the first large mammal brought to extinction as a result of human destruction to their natural habitat and resources."
—August Pfluger, CEO baiji.org Foundation

The ivory-billed woodpecker is a beautiful American bird that gives hope for threatened species. Entered into history books in the 1940s as "probably extinct," in 1999, more sightings of the bird began to surface. In 2000, the IUCN changed this woodpecker's status from probably extinct to critically endangered. There has been no confirmed record of the bird since 1944, however, and any living population is likely to be very small.

Sometimes called the "Good God bird" by awed onlookers, this woodpecker succumbed to forestry and agriculture. Conservationists and researchers continue to search for the bird in areas where it has allegedly been seen. In 2006, a $10,000 reward was offered for the discovery of a live ivory-billed woodpecker nest, roost, or feeding site, and in 2008, the Cornell Laboratory of Ornithology listed a reward of $50,000 to anyone who could deliver a live bird. While no one has earned the reward to date, we are hopeful that the bird is alive in small numbers and can be saved. Otherwise, it will likely once again be relisted as extinct.

"The bird became synonymous with extinction, a haunting reminder of what a culture may lose when it squanders its natural wealth."
—Scott Weidensaul, Smithsonian magazine

"For over 20 years, many agencies, conservation organizations, hunters and landowners have aggressively worked to conserve and restore the bottomland hardwood and swamp ecosystem. Now we know we must work even harder to conserve this critical habitat — not just for the ivory-billed woodpecker, but for the black bears and many other rare species of these unique woods."
Scott Simon, director of The Nature Conservancy of Arkansas.

Above: Birder's poster. Some experts believe this bird is already extinct.
Right: Recent photos of the ivory-billed woodpecker are very rare. Currently, only drawings do justice to the species.

Threat	10/10
Uniqueness	7/10
Human responsability	8/10
Hope	10/10
Symbolism	7/10
Average score	8.4/10

The Philippine eagle was dubbed "the world's noblest of fliers" by Charles Lindbergh. It is the world's largest eagle, with an impressive wingspan of over 180 cm (six feet). Unfortunately, it is no match for the massive machinery of the forestry industry. It is listed as a critically endangered species on the IUCN Red List because of its low numbers; fewer than 500 of the birds can be found in the wild.

Native to the Philippines, these eagles live on the island of Mindanao, with smaller populations found in eastern Luzon, Samar, and Leyte. They have been known to eat monkeys, however this is not their main source of food. The flying lemur makes up nearly 90 percent of the bird's diet. These eagles mate for life and both parents care for the young.

The existence of the Philippine eagle is precarious because of deforestation, pollution, and poaching, and the species' slow reproductive output. The CITES Appendices I and II have proposed various initiatives to protect this bird, and laws are in the works to prosecute poachers. There is hope that through public awareness campaigns, captive breeding programs, and sustainable development measures, the Philippine eagle will recover.

"The loss of this glorious bird would steal some of the world's wonder."
—Mel White, National Geographic

Above: Sign for the Philippine eagle release site.
Upper right: Logging work in the Philippine eagle's natural habitat.
Lower right: Individual in captivity.
Opposite page: The main threat for the species is the destruction of its natural habitat.

Threat   9/10
Uniqueness   9/10
Human responsability   8/10
Hope   8/10
Symbolism   8/10

Average score   8.4/10

Patrick Bonneville: This is not the king of the jungle as we know it, but a majestic little creature nonetheless. And it is about to lose its kingdom.

The black lion tamarin is a New World monkey, meaning it belongs to one of the five families of primates found in Central and South America. All of the black lion tamarins, about 1,000 individuals, live in eleven different regions of Brazil's Morro do Diabo State Park. Because some of these pockets are populated by fewer than 40 individuals, the black lion tamarin is listed as endangered.

Despite conservation efforts, these fragile monkey populations are at great risk. Road development through their natural habitat is shrinking the space available for them, and the tamarin must literally dodge cars to travel through its territory. Some experts are trying to devise plans, such as animal bridges, to curb inbreeding and allow isolated populations to spread out. In 1986, conservation efforts were stepped up, with reintroduction to the wild, translocation, and environmental education.

Opposite page: A golden lion tamarin baby, cousin of the black lion tamarin. It is also endangered.
Lower left: Close-up of a rare black lion tamarin.
Above: Captive black lion tamarin.

"Thirty years ago this species was on the brink of extinction. Now it has reached over 1,000 individuals, and is a conservation success story."
—Dr Garo Batmanian, WWF Brazil

Threat	10/10
Uniqueness	7/10
Human responsability	9.5/10
Hope	8/10
Symbolism	7/10
Average score	8.3/10

Some species of this New World monkey are on the verge of disappearing. Ka'apor, blonde, and golden-bellied capuchins are listed as critically endangered, while the robust tufted capuchin is evaluated as endangered.

Capuchins are considered the most intelligent of New World primates; they have been observed teaching their young to use tools, such as rocks, to smash open seed pods. Because of their intelligence, some have been trained to help people with reduced mobility, much in the same way as dogs are trained to assist humans. Capuchins are the monkey of choice for the exotic pet trade and are the monkeys seen with the organ grinder or as the jockey on the back of a racing greyhound.

Nearly all capuchins are arboreal and sleep high in trees. They are not picky about their forest surroundings, as long as they can find adequate food, shelter, and protection from their great number of predators. Known capuchin hunters include jaguars, cougars, coyotes, raptors, and even crocodiles.

It is widely accepted that the Ka'apor capuchin is the most threatened of all Amazonian primates. It is hunted for bushmeat and its habitat is being destroyed by development. The golden-bellied capuchin is also vulnerable to these threats; its population has declined by more than 80 percent over the past three generations.

To save the Ka'apor and golden-bellied capuchins, efforts in existing reserves must be amplified to halt the deforestation that deprives the monkeys of the fruit-bearing trees they eat from.

"Capuchin habitats are being fragmented and they are being lost to hunting for food and as 'pests' to crops."
—Animal Defenders International

Above: Mother and offspring in captivity.
Right: Capuchin standing tall. They can reach a height of 56 cm (22 in).

Threat	9/10
Uniqueness	8/10
Human responsability	8/10
Hope	8/10
Symbolism	8/10
Average score	8.2/10

The maned sloth is native to South America and is one of only four species of three-toed sloth. The IUCN Red List evaluates the maned sloth as an endangered species because of its low distribution, decline in habitat, and hunting.

The maned sloth is small, weighing up 4.5 kilograms (about 10 lbs). Curiously, its fur lays flat in the direction from foot to head so that when the sloth is hanging upside-down, its fur seems to lay like that of other mammals. It is a solitary creature that spends nearly all its time in trees, where it feeds on the leaves, buds, and soft twigs of only a few types of plants. Although walking is a chore for the sloth—it must drag itself along the ground—it is an able swimmer.

Its once-wide range has been reduced to a small area in eastern Brazil, in the Bahia coast forests; lumber extraction, charcoal production, hunting, and clearance for plantations and cattle pastures are scattering maned sloth populations.

In order to retain genetic diversity among the isolated groups, they need to be able to get to each other across clear-cut logging landscapes. Because sloths move so slowly, however, they are greatly exposed to danger and are often killed by oncoming traffic or dogs. The maned sloth is protected in Poço das Antas Biological Reserve, União Biological Reserve, and the Desengano State Park. It is vital that safe corridors be established between these colonies so they can mingle and reproduce in sufficient numbers to save themselves.

"Sloth – slow of movement, fond of sleep – was considered dim-witted, primitive, ill-adapted, and noteworthy only that it survived at all. It was not until the mid-twentieth century that scientists began uncovering the truth about this remarkable animal: rather than primitive, the sloth is one of the better adapted creatures on earth."
—The Sloth Sanctuary of Costa Rica

Threat	8/10
Uniqueness	8/10
Human responsability	8.5/10
Hope	7/10
Symbolism	9.5/10
Average score	8.2/10

Left: Three-toed sloth in its natural environment.
Right: Nursing and monitoring a baby sloth in Costa Rica, one of the last havens for the species.

The only true wild horse in existence today is known as Przewalski's horse or the Mongolian wild horse. Once considered extinct in the wild, it was reintroduced to its natural habitat in the early twentieth century in controlled areas in Mongolia. Current population groups in the wild are thought to number around 250. Przewalski's horse is listed as critically endangered on the IUCN Red List.

The wild horse predates recorded history and was common across western Europe and in Asia. Cave drawings depicting it have been dated to at least 20,000 BC. They depend on wild grasses and water for survival and are adapted for the harsh weather conditions of the arid deserts of China or the frigid plains of Mongolia.

The horse's habitat was degraded with the rise of agriculture and domestic farm animals, when their water sources dwindled and competition for food increased. Threats for today's reintroduced populations include disease, hybridization with domestic horses, and the resulting loss of genetic diversity. Hunting, military activity, climate change, and competition for resources also contribute to difficulties in maintaining sustainable populations.

Conservation supervisors in China focus on managing these occurrences and reducing their impact by wintering the Xinjiang group of wild horses in an enclosed pen. China's Wild Horse Breeding Centre at the Department of Forestry at Kalameili Nature Reserve in Xinjiang Uighur Autonomous Region aims to breed and reintroduce animals to the wild. In Mongolia, hunting the wild horse has been prohibited since 1930, and the animal is protected by law. In 1959 that country also created an international studbook to monitor the genetic integrity of captive horses reintroduced to the wild. Species survival plans for the horse also include efforts of zoos in Ukraine and Hungary, where wild horses are bred and studied to aid Mongolian conservation efforts.

Left: A small herd of wild horses in beautiful, rugged Mongolia.
Upper right: The Przewalski's Horse is the only truly wild horse.

Threat	6/10
Uniqueness	9/10
Human responsability	9/10
Hope	7.5/10
Symbolism	9.5/10
Average score	8.2/10

The addax is also known as the screwhorn antelope. Once found from northern Africa to Arabia and Israel, today there are fewer than 300 wild addax, found only in small territories of the Sahara Desert. A favorite of hunters in the twentieth century, their population has dwindled to such lows that they are now considered a critically endangered species on the IUCN Red List.

Both the male and female addax have spiraled horns that can reach lengths of up to 120 cm (47.25 inches). It is an ancient creature that has been depicted in Egyptian tombs as a domesticated animal.

Human encroachment is an important factor in the decline of addax populations, and because the remaining population groups are segregated, they are extremely vulnerable to hunters who prize addax for their fur, horns, and as trophies. While there are low numbers of addax in the wild, they are commonly found in captivity. These captive populations are generally kept for controlled trophy-hunting programs.

Threat	8.5/10
Uniqueness	8/10
Human responsability	8/10
Hope	7/10
Symbolism	9/10
Average score	8.1/10

Left: The addax is adapted to live in the desert. it lives in the Western Sahara desert.
Right: The addax has long black patches on the top of its head, between its spectacular spiraling horns.

The addax is listed in the CMS Appendix I and is included in the CMS Sahelo-Saharan Antelopes Action Plan. It is protected under national legislation in Morocco, Tunisia, and Algeria, and laws in Libya and Egypt forbid hunting of all gazelle species. Many reserves have been established to protect the addax in Algeria, Niger, Chad, and the Sudan; however, a lack of resources prevents them from being effective. There are plans to create other reserves in Chad and Niger as well as along the Mali-Mauritania border. In all cases, conservation measures will require the complete and dedicated cooperation of all nations.

Patrick Bonneville: The polar bear may seem scary, yet it is incredibly vulnerable. Its population is dropping at just about the same rate Antarctic ice is. The polar bear has become a strong symbol of the effects of climate change. We don't want it to become listed as "critically endangered". That would be too late.

This majestic animal is the world's largest land carnivore. The current population of polar bears in the wild is estimated at between twenty- and twenty-five thousand. Some 60 percent of the world's polar bears are found in Canada and the rest appear in other areas of the Arctic Circle including Greenland, Svalbard, Russia and Alaska. The biggest threat to these bears today is humanity, in the form of global warming. The IUCN Red List classes the polar bear as vulnerable.

Male polar bears can weigh up to 680 kilograms (1,500 lbs) and measure between two and three meters (6.5 - 9.8 ft) in length. The largest polar bear ever recorded weighed 1,200 kilograms (2,210 lbs). Although they have black skin under their fur that absorbs the sun's warmth, polar bears are so well insulated for their arctic environment that they need to move slowly to avoid overheating.

They are the top predator in the arctic marine ecosystem, but they are no match for hunters. European, Russian, and American hunters arrived in Arctic regions in the 1600s and hunted the polar bear greedily until the mid-1970s. In 1973, an international agreement put an end to uncontrolled hunting.

Many other significant factors make the polar bear vulnerable to extinction. Current climate trends due to global warming are reducing the arctic ice shelf. Some experts believe there will be no ice in Hudson Bay by 2080. The North is also receiving increasing amounts of industrial pollution from southern points. Many of these chemicals are lipophilic, or fat loving, and bond to the fat molecules of the polar bear's prey. Increased shipping and oil exploration are immediate sources of pollution that degrade the polar bear's territory; they also lead to increases in human-bear interaction.

Since polar bears are not fast reproducers and since there is no indication of a reduction of pollution-causing industry elsewhere in the world, experts agree that polar bears have a difficult road ahead of them.

"The listing of a currently healthy species based entirely on highly speculative and uncertain climate and ice modeling and equally uncertain and speculative modeling of possible impacts on a species would be unprecedented."
—*Alaska Governor Sarah Palin, 2007. Her administration filed suit against the federal government challenging the Interior Department's listing of the polar bear as "threatened."*

"Their habitat is melting. . . beautiful animals, literally being forced off the planet. They're in trouble, got nowhere else to go."
—*Al Gore*

Left: Polar bear mothers are known to take very good care of their offspring.
Above: A young girl watching a polar bear at a Canadian zoo. The polar bear is not yet listed as a endangered species in Canada. About 500 bears are killed per year by humans in northern Canada.
Right: Three polar bears approach the submarine USS Honolulu (SSN 718), 450 km (280 miles) from the North Pole, October 2003.

Threat	5/10
Uniqueness	9/10
Human responsability	9/10
Hope	7/10
Symbolism	10/10
Average score	8.0/10

Patrick Bonneville: This species has got to survive; its name gives us so much entertainment! On a more serious note, this donkey-like species lives in a troubled region of Africa where survival is difficult.

The scientific name of the African wild ass is Equus africanus, which indicates it is a member of the horse family; in fact, it is considered to be the ancestor of the domestic donkey. Once found in a wide area encompassing the Sudan, Egypt, and Libya, current wild adult populations in Eritrea and Ethiopia number no more than fifty adults each. This has led the IUCN to list the African wild ass as a critically endangered species.

Geography and humans are to blame for its decline. These animals inhabit a region known for drought. Humans hunt them to use their body parts for medicinal purposes. A third threat to the ass is inter-species breeding with the domestic donkey.

In 1969, Ethiopia established the Yangudi-Rassa National Park (4,731 km² or 1,827 mi) and the Mille-Serdo Wild Ass Reserve (8,766 km² or 3,385 mi) in an effort to help protect the animal. Unfortunately, the Ethiopian Wildlife Conservation Organization does not have the funding or the resources to manage the reserves. While conservationists claim that the population of the African wild ass has been stable for the past ten years, its tiny population does not leave much hope for a full repopulation of this region.

Above: The African wild ass weighs between 230-275 kg (500 - 600 lbs).
Right: The primary habitat of the African wild ass is arid and semi-arid bushland and grassland in north eastern Africa.

Threat	10/10
Uniqueness	8/10
Human responsability	8/10
Hope	7/10
Symbolism	7/10
Average score	8.0/10

The Siberian white crane is also called the snow crane. Known to follow long-ranging migratory routes to India, Iran, and China, this bird breeds in the wetlands of the Russian Arctic, in Yakutia, and in western Siberia. The Indian sub-population of this crane has not been observed since 2002. The IUCN has listed this long-range migratory bird as critically endangered.

The Siberian crane is dependent on the wetlands where it breeds, feeds, and winters. Its numbers are decreasing due to wetland degradation and loss caused by human activity and pollution. Pesticide use is also a significant cause of this crane's decline. Severe drought near China's Poyang Hu lake in 2003 and 2004 made living conditions for the crane difficult. China's proposed Three Gorges dam will alter the bird's winter grounds; if the development is less damaging than anticipated, the Siberian crane could be down-listed to endangered.

CITES Appendices I and II have designated legal protection for the Siberian crane in all range states. UNEP and the International Crane Foundation launched the Global Environmental Facility Siberian Crane project in 2003. This program will promote and develop protection programs and implement conservation efforts in the various wetlands that are home to the crane. These efforts to increase the population are similar to the North American efforts that successfully restored the whooping crane.

"It is pointless to restore the populations of Siberian Cranes unless their security can be provided along the migration route."
—The International Crane Foundation

Threat	9/10
Uniqueness	9/10
Human responsability	7.5/10
Hope	7/10
Symbolism	7.5/10
Average score	8.0/10

Right: Siberian white crane (grus leucogeranus) screeching guard call.
Opposite page: The Siberian crane is pure white except for its primary wing feathers, which are black.

The Luando Reserve and Cangandala National Park in Angola are vital grounds for the giant sable. Without these territories, the antelope falls victim to poaching and small-herd inbreeding. In August 2009, Angola's Ministry of Environment announced the adoption of the Giant Sable Antelope Project, with the goal of extending protection to the animal. The Angolan government also named the giant sable antelope a symbol of humanity.

The rare giant sable antelope is native to a small region in Angola, in south-central Africa. Shy by nature, this antelope was an innocent victim of the 1975-1991 Angolan Civil War, when an estimated 90 percent of its population was killed. The giant sable antelope is listed as critically endangered by the IUCN.

"Most locals worship the giant sable—they would not have survived if that were not the case. People really protect it; it is a sacred animal."
—Pedro Vaz Pinto, scientist who led a search to retrieve the giant sable antelope after the Angolan Civil War

At the end of the civil war, many feared the animal had been killed to extinction. When scientists discovered a new herd in July 2009, hopes grew that this majestic creature, the national symbol of Angola, could be saved. Today the IUCN reports a population of two to four hundred giant sable antelope. There are no known giant sable antelopes in captivity.

Left: Angolans worship the giant sable antelope. It is the pride of Angolan wild, the pride of a country and its people.
Above: As part of a conservation program, a female individual is translocated to a reserve.
Right: The giant sable antelope can only be found in Angola.

Threat	9/10
Uniqueness	8/10
Human responsability	8/10
Hope	7/10
Symbolism	8/10
Average score	8.0/10

Opposite page: The mountain tapir weighs between 150 and 225 kilograms (325 to 500 pounds). The females are larger than the males. **Left:** Mountain tapirs are found in 7 protected national parks in Colombia.

The mountain tapir is native to areas of South America and is related to other odd-toed ungulates, including horses and rhinoceroses. This woolly-coated animal can grow to to 225 kilograms (500 lbs) and can live for about thirty years. As a result of cattle introduction and habitat loss due to human interference and hunting, the mountain tapir is now extinct in most of its historical range. With an estimated 2,500 mature adults currently alive, the IUCN has listed the mountain tapir as an endangered species.

In countries like Ecuador, Peru, and Colombia, where domestic cattle are encroaching on wild ranges, the tapir leaves the area. Because females bear only one offspring at a time, reproduction rates are low in these scattered populations. The presence of war in much of its territory also has contributed to its demise, as conservationists are reluctant to risk their safety to visit mountain tapir ranges. Trade in mountain tapir skin for use in making backpacks, ropes, baskets means it is vulnerable to hunters. The animal's skin and feet are also used for traditional medicine.

Additional threats include poppy farming, conversion of grazing land into agricultural land, the development of hydroelectric dams, petroleum exploration, increased vehicle traffic, and human expansion. This simple animal has major hurdles to overcome before its link on the chain is secured.

"The primary threats to the mountain tapir are warfare and habitat loss due to poppy farming and growth of ranching and agriculture, driven by human population growth in the Andean region."
—Tapir Specialist Group, part of the IUCN Species Survival Commission

"Major mining interests are poised to take over these last mountain tapir cloud forest homes."
—The Andean Tapir Fund

Threat	8/10
Uniqueness	8/10
Human responsability	9/10
Hope	7.5/10
Symbolism	7.5/10
Average score	8.0/10

The lemur is a primate that lives on Madagascar and surrounding islands. Of the different types of lemurs known, ten are considered critically endangered, seven are endangered, and nineteen are considered vulnerable. An estimated 80 percent of lemur habitat has been destroyed. All subspecies are protected from hunt or capture for trade by CITES.

The word "lemur" means "spirits of the night," a name probably bestowed because of this creature's large reflective eyes and cries in the dark. Lemurs eat fruits, flowers, and leaves as well as insects, spiders, and small vertebrates. All but one subspecies, the Indri, have long tails which are used to communicate, swing in trees, and keep balance. Most lemur subspecies live in matriarchal groups and are primarily arboreal. Only the ring-tailed lemur spends any significant amount of time on the ground. Like their long-distance primate cousins, lemurs have opposable thumbs.

In 2008, there were ninety-nine living lemur species. Conservation is a priority in Madagascar, but resources and funding needed to ensure projects are insufficient. The Duke Lemur Center and Idea Wild are active in conservation efforts, specifically in the prevention of deforestation. Idea Wild works with farmers to establish sustainable methods of farming instead of traditional slash and burn practices.

"Illegal logging of precious wood has emerged as one of the most severe threats to Madagascar's dwindling northeastern rainforests."
—Erik Patel, Cornell University

Above: A ring-tailed lemur family.
Upper right: A brown orange lemur lies on a branch in the Madagascar wild.
Opposite page: The ring-tailed lemur or lemur catta is the most recognized lemur due to its long black and white ringed tail and its orange eyes.

Threat	6/10
Uniqueness	9.5/10
Human responsability	8.5/10
Hope	6/10
Symbolism	10/10
Average score	8.0/10

The Mediterranean monk seal is widely thought to be the world's rarest pinniped, or fin-footed mammal. It is one of the six most threatened mammal species in the world. It has a current population of about 500 individuals and is listed as critically endangered on the IUCN Red List. Most of these animals are scattered throughout a wide range, from the Mediterranean Sea to the eastern Atlantic Ocean near the Tropic of Cancer.

The monk seal lives to be about twenty and can reproduce from about age four. In the past, open beaches were the habitat of choice for this seal. Easy prey, they were hunted to the point where they have retreated to undersea caves to mate and give birth. Most scientists agree that this is a behavioral adaptation that allows them to avoid contact with human activity. There is evidence, however, that many seal pups do not survive birth in these relatively inaccessible caves, because of the dangerous, sharp rocks of these rugged locations.

The largest surviving colony is found in Cabo Blanco, in the Atlantic Ocean. In the summer of 1997, two-thirds of this colony was killed within two months. The exact cause is unknown but it is thought that phytoplanktonic toxins or a virus were likely to blame. This was proof of the species' vulnerability. Today, at Cabo Blanco, there are about 150 seals, about half the population of ten years ago. If another virus were to hit, this mammal could very well be exterminated.

The historical enemy of this seal was hunting, today its main threats come from inadvertent damage from fishing equipment, marine pollution, and habitat fragmentation.

The Mediterranean monk seal is legally protected throughout its range. Two areas in particular have been established for conservation: the Desertas Islands in the Madeira archipelago and the Northern Sporades Islands National Marine Park in Greece. Both hope to see an improvement in population numbers and density. The ideal recovery would entail a return to colony groups that can gather on beaches.

Threat	9/10
Uniqueness	4/10
Human responsability	9.5/10
Hope	8.5/10
Symbolism	8.5/10
Average score	7.9/10

Left: A very rare photo of a wild Mediterranean monk seal, taken in Greece.

Sometimes known as the black ape, this macaque lives in northeastern Indonesia on the island of Sulawesi and other smaller islands. The IUCN considers the Celebes crested macaque critically endangered, based on the drastic decline in its population during the past forty years. The 100,000-strong population on the island of Pulau Bacan is not calculated in the IUCN evaluation, since the macaques were reintroduced there and have become a pest on that island.

On the island of Sulawesi, the macaque population hovers between 4,000 and 6,000 individuals. It is often killed as a pest because it is fond of crops and can destroy farmed fields. It is also hunted as bushmeat. Conservation efforts include a "Save the Yaki" program—as this macaque is known locally—involving Indonesian and foreign partners, as well as off-site breeding programs in several European zoos.

Upper right: Mother nurses offspring for a year.
Below: A celebes crested macaque family.

"There is urgent action needed to stop the encroachment into protected areas especially Tangkoko, which represents the most likely viable natural remaining population of the species to survive."
—IUCN's Red List Program

Threat	9/10
Uniqueness	7/10
Human responsability	8/10
Hope	8/10
Symbolism	7.5/10
Average score	7.9/10

The saola is an extremely rare bovine that was discovered in 1992 in Southeast Asia. Initial reports documented only eleven individuals, but other reports estimate their numbers to be in the low hundreds. They are considered critically endangered by the IUCN.

Little is known about this mountain and forest-dwelling animal that is found near the border of Laos and Vietnam. DNA studies show that it is related to the bovine species, similar to the ox, cow, and antelope. They shy away from human activity, and all efforts to keep the saola in captivity have failed. Because they are reclusive, they are difficult to study. It is known that hunting and increases in the number of roads are almost certainly having a negative impact on saola populations. Even if the saola is not directly targeted by hunters, it is often killed accidentally during the hunt for other game whose body parts are destined for use in Chinese medicine.

The protection of this animal is a priority for local governments, and the WWF has been active in the saola's protection since its discovery only a few years ago.

"The saola acts as an emblem of conservation efforts in Vietnam, yet it remains on the brink of extinction."
—Tran Minh Hien, WWF Vietnam's Programme Director

Vietnam

Threat	8/10
Uniqueness	9/10
Human responsability	8/10
Hope	8/10
Symbolism	6/10
Average score	7.8/10

Above: The saola can only be found in Ha Tinh province, near the Laos border.
Right: Photo of a saola head, taken in Vietnam.

Patrick Bonneville: America is on the right path to save the red wolf.

The red wolf is native to North America, where studies show it was once common from Texas to Florida, with recent research showing proof of red wolf populations as far north as eastern Canada. By 1980, they were extinct in the wild. At that time, the United States Fish and Wildlife Service began a mission to bring them back. There are now some 150 red wolves in the wild. IUCN's Red List labels them as critically endangered.

Today, they can be found only in North Carolina, where they were reintroduced. It is not known if there are any populations outside the protected region in that state.

Threat	9/10
Uniqueness	7/10
Human responsability	8/10
Hope	7/10
Symbolism	8/10
Average score	7.8/10

Continuing threats are hybridization with coyotes and human interference. Newly introduced wolves were killed by vehicles on roads, but it is hoped that subsequent generations of wolves have learned to avoid such dangerous travel areas.

Hope remains that this species will be saved from complete extinction and once again range broadly in the wild.

"Once common throughout the southeastern United States, red wolf populations were decimated by the 1960s due to intensive predator control programs and loss of habitat."
—U.S. Fish and Wildlife Service

Upper left: The red wolf is slighty bigger than a coyote. A young red wolf could look like a coyote.
Above: Individuals are monitored with a radio transmitter that emits pulse signals.

The slender-billed vulture is a native bird of India, Bangladesh, south Nepal, and West Bengal. According to the IUCN Red List, it is a critically endangered species. In the past, the bird's range also included many countries of Southeast Asian where it is now extinct or extremely rare.

This vulture lives within the boundaries of human habitat and scavenges for carrion along highways, at garbage dumps, and near slaughterhouses. It is a social creature that prefers communal living. It breeds far from villages and makes its nest high in treetops. In India and elsewhere, vultures are an important link in the ecosystem, as they dispose of both human and animal remains.

The species has suffered a severe population decline because of poisoning from the veterinary use of the anti-inflammatory drug diclofenac. Around the year 2000, reports of alarming numbers of dead slender-billed vultures began appearing in Nepal, Pakistan, and India. As scavengers, the vultures were feeding on the carcasses of livestock treated with the drug; they then suffered renal failure. Other smaller factors affecting the bird's population include human consumption, pesticides, and the absence of livestock carcasses to feed on.

Above: Slender-billed vulture in captivity, in India.

In an effort to stabilize the decline of the slender-billed vulture, India has banned the manufacture, but not the usage, of diclofenac. Similar conditions exist in Nepal and Pakistan. Drug companies are developing alternative medicines to treat livestock for pain, fever, and inflammation, and initial reports show no negative impact of these drugs on vultures.

In Cambodia, there is a unique initiative called the Vulture Conservation Project, which funds feeding programs for the birds through eco-tourist attractions featuring "vulture restaurants." Other conservation projects exist, including a captive breeding program in India, as well as tagging and monitoring programs that will allow researchers a greater understanding of the vulture's range, site fidelity, and habitat preferences.

Threat	9/10
Uniqueness	7/10
Human responsability	8/10
Hope	8/10
Symbolism	7/10
Average score	7.8/10

Left: The Galapagos cormorant's wings are too small for flight.

The Galapagos cormorant is very vulnerable to natural disasters, such as ocean storms, and climatic events such as El Niño. Man-made interference threatens the bird as well, as oil spills and tourism are serious threats to its habitat. It is also victimized by non-native animals, such as cats and rats, that have been introduced to the islands— its inability to fly means it cannot easily escape threats.

Patrick Bonneville: Tourism is going to kill the marvels of this archipelago. All human activities should be forbidden; Charles Darwin would agree with that.

Conservationists are concerned by the bird's fluctuating numbers. It is now only found in two small regions. The lowest recorded population was in 1983, following an El Niño season, when there were only 400 birds. Today's population appears to be relatively stable, with some 1,400 birds on the islands. It is essential that the population be maintained at a number that will allow pairs to continue to reproduce.

Also known as the flightless cormorant, this bird is native to the Galapagos Islands and is the only cormorant species that cannot fly. According to the IUCN Red List, it is endangered because of its restricted range, small population, and environmental and human threats.

This bird has webbed feet and strong legs for swimming, although its wings lack the musculature that would permit it to fly. It feeds on fish, eels, small octopuses, and the like. Cormorants are seabirds, but their feathers are not waterproof; air trapped between their feathers prevents them from becoming waterlogged, and they dry their feathers in the sun. They form small groups of only a few pairs and have no fear of humans.

"There are 29 species of cormorants that live throughout the world, but the flightless cormorant can only be found in the Galapagos Islands and is the only one that cannot fly."
—The Galapagos Conservation Trust

Threat	9/10
Uniqueness	7/10
Human responsability	8/10
Hope	7/10
Symbolism	8/10
Average score	7.8/10

The angel shark is found in waters off Great Britain and, rarely, in the Mediterranean. In 2006, the species was declared extinct in the North Sea. The IUCN Red List classifies it as critically endangered, a downward move for the angel shark—in 2000, it was only considered vulnerable to extinction.

Angel sharks prefer temperate waters and are bottom dwellers who bury their flat bodies in sediment as they wait for prey to pass. Because they remain on the ocean floor, they are often victims of bottom trawling, set nets, and bottom long-line fishing equipment.

Historically, this shark was abundant in western European waters. Its population began to dwindle with the arrival of commercial fishing trawlers. Often marketed as monkfish, it is also used to make oil and fishmeal. Its low reproduction rate further weakens its precarious position on the edge of extinction. Populations around the Canary Islands and North Africa seem to be healthy, however more research is needed to confirm this trend. Although the angel shark is protected in the three marine reserves of the Balearic Islands, no sightings have been reported there since the mid 1990s.

Threat	8/10
Uniqueness	6/10
Human responsability	9.5/10
Hope	8/10
Symbolism	7.5/10
Average score	7.8/10

Other conservation efforts include the Mediterranean International Trawl Survey and protection through the 1976 Barcelona Convention, in which British law also aims to reduce pollution in waters off England and Wales. The United Kingdom and Belgium have also advocated for the angel shark by demanding it be listed in the Convention for the Protection of the Marine Environment's North-East Atlantic priority list of threatened and endangered species.

"Before 1978, angel sharks were usually thrown back when caught. But this changed dramatically when a Santa Barbara fish processor decided to promote the angel shark as a tasty morsel."
—Monterey Bay Aquarium Foundation

Above: The angel shark is often referred as the "sand devil."

The reclusive Amur leopard is native to the far easternmost regions of Russia. It is one of the rarest felines in the world, with an estimated thirty-five to forty individuals remaining in the wild. It is listed as critically endangered, and some experts believe that this animal is on the brink of extinction.

This leopard subspecies is specifically adapted to life in the cold, harsh climates of Russia. It grows a long coat for winter months and has longer legs than other leopards, most likely an environmental adaptation for walking through the deep snow. It is a nocturnal and solitary creature with a habit of hiding its prey so it cannot be taken by another predator. It is reported that this leopard can make leaps of more than six meters (over 19 feet).

The leopard lost a whopping 80 percent of its habitat between 1970 and 1983 to logging, forest fires, and farming. Thirteen international and Russian non-governmental agencies have pooled their resources in an effort to save the Amur leopard. The coalition is called the Amur Leopard and Tiger Alliance and helps protect the leopard from poaching and habitat loss. ALTA members also conduct education and outreach programs in an effort to bring attention to the animal's dire situation. Some experts believe that the remaining leopards could be transplanted to other northern forests where they can thrive, however the uncertainty of an adequate food supply remains.

"A poorly managed reorganization of the protected area in the range of the critically-endangered Amur leopard has left a key Russian reserve without protection and even the most basic funds to fight fires and poaching."
—*The Zoological Society of London*

Above: The coat of the amur leopard is 7.5 cm (3 in) thick in winter.
Right: In the wild, leopards can live up to 15 years.

Threat	9/10
Uniqueness	7.5/10
Human responsability	9/10
Hope	7/10
Symbolism	6/10
Average score	7.7/10

Challenges to the survival of the wild camel include hunting, inter-breeding, and degradation of their natural territory. Industries such as mining, agriculture, gas pipelines, and associated industrial developments have had a negative impact on the population, and conservationists expect to see a loss of twenty-five to thirty animals yearly. An additional threat comes in the form of wolf attacks, which have increased in recent years.

This native to northeastern Asia has been domesticated to the point of near extinction. While there are some 1.4 million domesticated Bactrian camels, there are fewer than 1,000 left in the wild. They were listed as critically endangered by the IUCN in 2002.

The wild Bactrian camel can be found on the border of China and Mongolia, where summer daytime temperatures can soar to forty degrees Celsius and winter temperatures can plummet to minus forty. They store fat in their two humps as a water and energy source, since fresh water is difficult for them to find. It is widely accepted that the Bactrian camel dates to prehistoric times, as shown by numerous cave paintings. It is also known that Asian societies used the camel in caravans as many as 3,000 years ago.

As this animal is a food source for miners in the region it inhabits, education programs are necessary to ensure its survival. Thirty percent of its territory in Mongolia is under special protection, however with an estimated 80 percent reduction in population forseen for the next fifty years, the wild Bactrian camel has much to overcome.

"Scientists have every reason to think a detailed study of the immune system of the wild Bactrian camel will yield scientific discoveries which will be of benefit to the whole of mankind."
—The Wild Camel Protection Foundation

Threat	10/10
Uniqueness	7/10
Human responsability	8.5/10
Hope	6.5/10
Symbolism	6.5/10
Average score	7.7/10

Left: Close-up of the curly Bactrian camel.
Above: Herd of wild camels in Mongolia.

Patrick Bonneville: This is a magnificient creature. It is one of the natural treasures found wild in Madagascar. The natural world in this area needs to be better protected. According to experts, this tortoise will not make to the next century. It might actually have only 20 years left. Why? Because of us.

This tortoise wears a astonishing pattern on its shell. Yellow lines radiate from the center of each dark plate of the tortoise's carapace. The radiated tortoise is found only in the southern part of Madagascar, with a few exception in the nearby island of Réunion. Its carapace is around 41 cm (16 in) long and the animal weighs up to 16 kg (35 pounds).

No recent estimates of wild populations are available but the population is certainly declining. It has become much more rare to see wild individuals, and their natural habitat is being devasted. Even though their life span can be quite long, over 50 years, their survival is very uncertain. According to IUCN, the causes of their habitat loss include deforestation for use as agricultural land, the grazing of livestock, and the burning of wood for charcoal.

Short-term thinking on the part of humans is jeopardizing the survival of this great Madagascar tortoise, probably the most beautiful one in the world. This species is not ready to give up. When caught, the radiated tortoise emits very high-pitched cries for hours. It is the only defense they now have.

"The rate of hunting of radiated tortoises is similar to the hunting pressure on American bison during the early 19th century, where they were nearly hunted to extinction when they once numbered in the tens of millions."
- Brian D. Horne, Wildlife Conservation Society

Above: A fairly large example of one of the most beautifully decorated tortoises in the world.

"I can't think of a tortoise species that has undergone a more rapid rate of decline in modern times, or a more drastic contraction in range, than the radiated tortoise."
—Rick Hudson, president of the Turtle Survival Alliance

Threat	7.5/10
Uniqueness	7/10
Human responsability	8/10
Hope	8/10
Symbolism	8/10
Average score	7.7/10

This bird lives on the island of Grenada in the Lesser Antilles and is one of the most critically endangered doves in the world. Currently there are only 180 alive. The IUCN lists the bird as critically endangered.

Grenada's economy, as with that of other tropical islands, relies heavily on tourism, and hotel resort developments have affected the bird's numbers. Natural disasters, such as hurricanes, have also been a threat to the dove population.

While the government of Grenada has taken clear measures to conserve the island's national bird, a recent proposal to sell state land for the development of a hotel at the Mount Hartman Estate has engendered some controversy. The proposed resort is in a park previously designated as a dove protection zone. BirdLife International, the American Bird Conservancy, and noteworthy private individuals such as Margaret Atwood and Graeme Gibson have spoken out against the development.

Above: Rare photo of a Grenada Dove.

While the government assures conservationists of a "win-win" situation, it is essential that they follow through with their engagement to protect the Grenada dove by strictly enforcing conservation criteria before any project is approved.

"Four Seasons Hotels and Resorts, renowned for providing the rich and famous with luxury getaways, is facing criticism from bird lovers for its plans to build a new resort that will destroy the last stronghold of the critically endangered Grenada Dove."
—American Bird Conservancy

"There's a terrible irony in the government's willingness to critically compromise the continued existence of the Grenada Dove - which as the island's National Bird is a symbol of the country's distinctiveness and its culture - simply to provide sea-views to people from away."
—Margaret Atwood & Graeme Gibson, Honorary Patrons of BirdLife's Rare Bird Club

Threat	9/10
Uniqueness	5/10
Human responsability	9.5/10
Hope	7/10
Symbolism	8/10
Average score	7.7/10

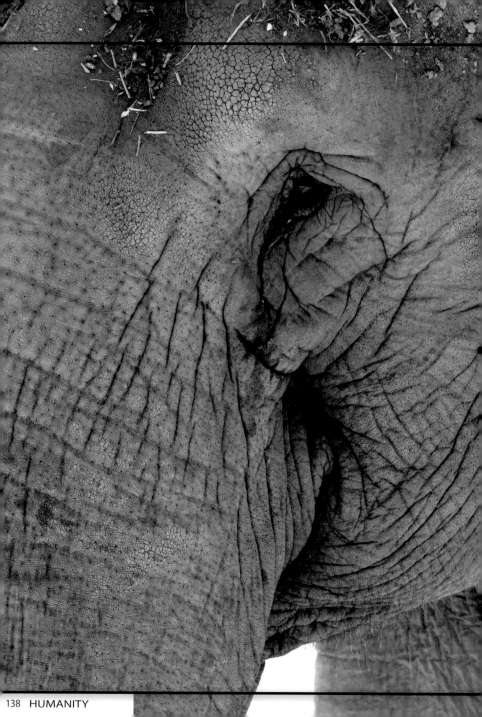

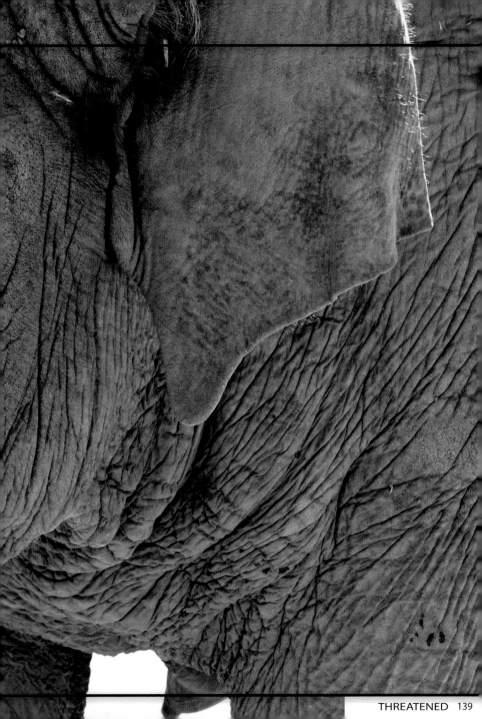

Patrick Bonneville: Its cousin, the mammoth, is gone. Let's make sure we can save all elephant species. Let's make sure our kids know what we're talking about when we read them stories about these big, gentle creatures.

This elephant is Asia's largest living land animal. The IUCN has listed it as an endangered species, and experts estimate the population in the wild to be between 25,000 and 52,000—a decline of 50 percent in the last 60 years. They are now extinct in west Asia, Java, and most of China.

Wild Asian elephants are found in Bangladesh, India, Sri Lanka, Indochina, Nepal, Indonesia, and Thailand. Domesticated elephants are abundant, doing work similar to the bull or cow in North American cultures. Although the Asian elephant is slightly smaller than its African relative, it still weighs an incredible 3,000 to 5,000 kilograms (6,500 to 11,000 lbs). The female rarely has visible tusks.

Several challenges face the Asian elephant. Wild Asian elephants travel through ancient migratory paths, but as humans replace those paths with villages, the elephants become lost and vulnerable to poaching. They are killed by hunters for their ivory tusks, meat, and hides.

The WWF touts the Asian elephant as a flagship species. This means that efforts to conserve its populations in the wild, over a wide area, will help guarantee protection for all animals and plants in those regions. The long-term future of the Asian elephant lies in the creation of protected zones through specific conservation programs such as the WWF's Asian Rhinos and Elephants Action Strategy.

Below: Elephants for sale at Asia's largest cattle fair, in Sonepur, Bihar, India.
Right: Close-up of the the largest living land animals, now threated with extinction.

Threat	5/10
Uniqueness	10/10
Human responsability	8/10
Hope	5/10
Symbolism	10/10
Average score	7.6/10

"Myanmar has the potential to become a major stronghold for Asian elephants; it's a pity that illegal capture and killing are pushing elephants towards extinction there. Neighboring countries need to seriously reconsider their policy on the use of captive elephants and also enforce laws to stop illegal trade in wildlife products."
—Ajay Desai, Co-Chair of the IUCN Asian Elephant Specialist Group

The African wild dog is often called Africa's "painted wolf." Historically found in thirty-nine countries, only fifteen African countries have wild dog populations today. Total numbers are estimated at between 3,000 and 5,500, which has resulted in an IUCN Red List classification as an endangered species.

Wild dogs live in packs throughout sub-Saharan Africa, where they prey on a variety of animals. Their role as a predator means they hold an important place in the structure and function of various ecosystems.

Wild dogs are carnivores that require large areas to roam and ecologically diverse spaces in order to survive. There are two major threats to these criteria for survival: people and predators. Interference from humans, especially as farmers kill them out of fear for their livestock, is a significant factor. There have even been petitions circulated to wipe the species off the face of the earth for the good of all other creatures in Africa. Predators, such as lions and hyenas, are in direct competition with the African wild dog for food, and lions will kill dogs in order to save food stocks for themselves. Hyenas eat the dogs the lions kill. While under normal conditions predators do not extinguish a species' population, the wild dog is vulnerable because of its already reduced numbers.

Conservationists aim to educate people at the grassroots level about the impact of their aggression toward the African wild dog. Unfortunately, there is little coordination in conservation efforts between the countries that consitute the dog's range.

"Wild dogs were actively destroyed by wildlife managers in most areas until the later part of the 20th century, due to a perception that their method of killing prey was cruel, and that their cursorial hunting methods were disruptive to antelope populations. Beginning in the 1970's, culling of wild dogs came to an end, and they are now legally protected in the seven nations that hold substantial numbers."
- African Wild Dog Conservation

"Population size is continuing to decline as a result of ongoing conflict with human activities, infectious disease, habitat fragmentation."
—IUCN

Threat	8/10
Uniqueness	8/10
Human responsability	7/10
Hope	6/10
Symbolism	9/10
Average score	7.6/10

Right: The African wild dog is also known as the painted hunting dog or the African hunting dog.

Left: A Hawaiian monk seal napping on a beach.
Below: Sign on a beach. This species is higly protected in Hawaii.

The U.S. Marine Mammal Protection Act of 1973 has provided for the seal in that almost all its habitat is within protective boundaries where human activity is either prohibited or strictly controlled. Current conservation efforts are focused on monitoring fishing and the presence of toxic chemicals.

The Hawaiian monk seal is the most endangered of all seals. The IUCN lists it as critically endangered due to its rapid decline in population and because of continued threats to its existence despite ongoing conservation efforts.

Known to natives as ilio-holo-i-ka-uaua, or the "dog that runs in rough waters," this seal was awarded the title of Hawaii's official mammal on June 11, 2008 in an effort to bring attention to its fragile status. Hawaiian monk seals are non-migratory, which means they are born and live within a relatively small region.

Conservationists only partially understand why this population is in decline and fear that the trend might not be reversible. Estimates show that the population could drop to 200 individuals within the next two decades.

"The endangered Hawaiian monk seal, a biological treasure unique to the Hawaiian Archipelago, is in crisis. Despite living mostly in the now relatively protected environment of the Northwestern Hawaiian Islands, the monk seal population has declined steadily and is at its lowest level in recorded history."
—The Pacific Islands Fisheries Science Center

Threat	9/10
Uniqueness	6/10
Human responsability	9/10
Hope	7/10
Symbolism	7/10
Average score	7.6/10

The Adriatic salmon is found in freshwater rivers of Bosnia and Herzegovina, Croatia, Serbia, and Montenegro. The species is often referred as the Adriatic trout or as the softmouth trout. It is listed as an endangered species on the IUCN Red List because of severe habitat loss, sportfishing, commercial fishing, and hybridization with introduced trout.

Its desirability as a game fish means its extremely small population continues to decline. Other threats include hydroelectric dam projects and water pollution. There are no known current conservation efforts.

"This past summer, a scientific team returned to the Zeta, on a tip that a single man was protecting a population of these native fish in a tributary where a spring bubbled full force from the ground. Sure enough, because of the efforts of this one man who lived on the river, they were still there, a total population numbering in the hundreds."
—James Prosek, co-founder of the World Trout Initiative, about the survival of the "Adriatic trout".

Threat	9/10
Uniqueness	4/10
Human responsability	9/10
Hope	9/10
Symbolism	7/10
Average score	7.6/10

Above: The Adriatic salmon in its habitat.
Left: Neretva river near in Mostar, Bosnia and Herzegovina. The Neretva river is one of the rare rivers where the Adriatic salmon still swims.

"*Extinction of the species is a possibility within the next two decades unless disease spread can be stopped.*"
—*University of Adelaide zoologist Dr. Jeremy Austin, 2008*

Threat	7.5/10
Uniqueness	9/10
Human responsability	5/10
Hope	6/10
Symbolism	10/10
Average score	7.5/10

The Tasmanian devil is a carnivorous marsupial that can only be found on the island of Tasmania. Its population has been severely decimated by a form of cancer, and today this creature is listed by the IUCN as endangered.

After the extinction of the Thylacine in 1936, the Tasmanian devil became the largest carnivorous marsupial in the world. Devils have a well-documented reputation for their odor, aggression, and the noise they make. They are solitary animals but can be found in small groups, especially when eating. They devour every bit of a carcass—bones, fur, and flesh—and in their eating they make so much noise that they can be heard several kilometers away.

This creature's main threat is devil facial tumor disease (DFTD), an extremely aggressive form of non-viral parasitic cancer that was first recorded in 1996 in Australia. Unlike cancer's usual modus operandi, this strain is transmitted from one devil to the next. In the years following DFTD's first appearance, the devil population dropped by an estimated 50 percent. In regions where there were many individuals, the disease killed 100 percent of the population within eighteen months.

Some experts have estimated that the devil will be extinct within twenty years. The Tasmanian government launched the Tasmanian Devil Disease Program in 2003. This program intends to research, examine, and speculate on the disease, its process, and possible cures. In the January 2010 issue of *Science*, researchers linked DFTD to the Schwann cells in the devils' peripheral nervous system. This news has increased conservationists' hopes of finding a cure.

"While it appears that we haven't caused this particular disease within devils, we know that humanity in general places a lot of pressure on wildlife. So if there's any way that we can help to correct that, then I want to be part of it."
—Internationally-renowned nature photographer Darran Leal

Left: The Tasmanian devil has the strongest bite of any living mammal, thanks to its powerful jaw.
Right: The Tasmanian devil is part of Australian culture and heritage. It is a strong iconic animal for the country and it is the symbol of the Tasmanian National Parks and Wildlife Service.

This green parrot is native to the archipelago of Puerto Rico. It is called Iguaca by the indigenous Taíno people, whose pronunciation of the name sounds like the call of the bird. According to the IUCN Red List, the bird is critically endangered.

The Puerto Rican parrot was first described in European literature in 1783. Because nearly all its natural mangrove and lowland habitat has been destroyed, the parrot now lives in forests at elevations of 200 to 600 meters. The wild birds will now only nest and lay their eggs in man-made tree cavities.

The bird's survival is threatened by parasitic botflies, predators, and natural disasters, such as hurricanes. Its natural habitat is now a mere 0.2 percent of what it once was; this area is now protected in the Caribbean National Forest. By 1975, only thirteen Puerto Rican Amazons were alive, although since then conservation efforts have proven effective and the current population of about forty birds is reported as stable. Efforts to ensure a continuation of this trend include reintroducing birds from captivity to the wild and tracking them with radio-telemetry.

Above: The Puerto Rican parrot reproduces only once a year, a behavior that does not help its endangered situation.

"Upon the arrival of Columbus to Puerto Rico in 1493, the Puerto Rican Parrot numbered approximately a million birds. By the 1930's that number had reduced to approximately 2000 birds. By 1954 to an estimated 200 birds. By 1964 to 70 birds."
—Dr. Mark L. Stafford, Parrots International

Threat	8.5/10
Uniqueness	5/10
Human responsability	9/10
Hope	8/10
Symbolism	7/10
Average score	7.5/10

The four subspecies of the rainforest-dwelling black-crested gibbon are listed as critically endangered on the IUCN Red List. Populations of this ape have decreased by over 80 percent in the past forty-five years because of habitat loss and hunting. It is estimated that there are only between 1,300 and 2,000 of them left in the wild.

A native of Southeast Asia, the black-crested gibbon is remarkable for the way it swings through tree-tops from branch to branch. Monogomous pairs procreate only once every two to three years and sing together every morning to reinforce their pair-bond and to announce the family group's presence to the area.

Below: Males are almost completely black and females are more golden with variable black patches, including a black streak on the head.
Upper right: The gibbon's habit of swinging under branches is known as brachiating.

Deforestation and hunting for bushmeat and traditional medicines are the primary causes for its near-extinction status. The black-crested gibbon is protected by the CITES Appendix I trade ban, and, in Lao PDR, measures to control hunting and steep fines for trade are in place. Regions in the Wuliang mountain range are designated as protected, and conservationists are lobbying for northern Vietnam's Che Tao Forest, the last safe spot for this gibbon, to be established as a reserve.

"The black-crested gibbons of Vietnam and China are among the rarest primates in the world."
—IUCN/SSC Primate Specialist Group

Threat	7/10
Uniqueness	7/10
Human responsability	8/10
Hope	8/10
Symbolism	7.5/10
Average score	7.5/10

Like some creature from a movie set, the Chinese giant salamander is the largest in the world. Once upon a time these giant salamanders grew up to 180 centimeters (6 ft). Today, they are slightly smaller. In the past forty-five years, their numbers have dropped by 80 percent because of habitat loss, pollution, over-collection, over-fishing, and hunting for medicinal purposes. The IUCN Red List considers them critically endangered.

Chinese giant salamanders live in rocky mountain streams and lakes throughout China. They feed on insects, frogs, and fish. They are near-blind and rely on sensors that run the length of their bodies to detect food and other vibrations.

This is a commercially exploited species. It is part of the Chinese diet and has been over-fished for decades. It is under continued threat of habitat loss, especially due to the damming of rivers; damming changes the quality and course of water. This can segregate individuals, and reproduction drops as a result. A third serious threat is water pollution from the mining industry.

Above: Exploring Wulingyuan National Park in Hunan, China.
Right: Fossil of a Chinese giant salamander dispalyed in Baden, Germany.

China has placed the giant salamander under protection by law. Captive rearing programs are currently in place, but unfortunately the vast majority of salamanders raised in these programs end up being sold on the open market instead of being reintroduced into the wild. There is no documentation to support the reported success of captive breeding programs.

The Zhangjiajie Giant Salamander Nature Reserve, however, is dedicated to saving the species. At the park, regular surveys are conducted to establish the location of viable populations so that protective measures can be implemented. The reserve is also active in both community conservation and education initiatives.

"Their meat is considered a delicacy in China, as well as a source for traditional medicines. Since the 1960's, it is estimated that 80% of their prior populations have died off."
—Amanda Miller, Green Daily

Threat	8/10
Uniqueness	10/10
Human responsability	7/10
Hope	7/10
Symbolism	5/10
Average score	7.4/10

Left: Terpsiphone corvina (Seychelles Paradise flycatcher) on La Digue island in the Seychelles.

The Seychelles Paradise-flycatcher is endemic to the Seychelles, a group of islands off the northern tip of Madagascar. The species is considered critically endangered because of its extremely small range and population decline. Estimates put its population count at about 100 individuals.

This rare bird lives on insects, larvae, and spiders, which it catches in flight or from a perch. They are clever builders who use twigs, palm fiber, and even spider webs to create their oval-shaped nests.

Tourism is the main source of revenue for the Seychelles, but unfortunately it is also the main threat for the Seychelles paradise-flycatcher. As hotel and residential development projects spring up, the bird's territory is reduced. Habitat loss is also occurring because of trees being cut down to limit certain plant diseases. The introduction of non-native fauna is also a threat to the bird.

Habitat management has helped stabilize the population over the past couple of decades, and the bird enjoys some safety in the dense forests of the Veuve Nature Reserve. In order to help the species survive, a small, mature woodland area was established as a nature reserve on La Digue in 1991. Here, staff members monitor the bird's status and operate an education center and public awareness programs. As well as implementing habitat and predator protection programs, conservationists monitor pollution. They also introduced a wetland and ground water protection program when a new landfill site was established.

"It would be a remarkable achievement to bring the last Seychelles endemic out of imminent danger of extinction."
—Dr Stuart Butchart, BirdLife's Global Species Programme Coordinator

Threat	8/10
Uniqueness	8/10
Human responsability	8/10
Hope	7/10
Symbolism	6/10
Average score	7.4/10

The commercial and sport fishing industries nearly wiped the species out. By the 1970s, the California State Department of Fish and Game realized that the giant sea bass was in serious trouble and put the fish under protection in 1982. It has been under partial protection in Mexico since 1992. Conservationists report an increase in the overall population, however there is no documentation to support these claims.

Also known as the black sea bass, this huge fish is native to the Pacific Ocean. By 1996, the IUCN had evaluated the fish as critically endangered on its Red List.

The giant sea bass was quite common in the waters around Southern California, the Gulf of California, and the Humboldt Bay regions. It can be found as far west as Japan. It prefers relatively shallow ocean waters, although it has been recorded in the high sea. Little is known about its behavior, although its size makes rare sightings memorable. The biggest specimen ever photographed was caught in 2007 by a Mexican fisherman. It weighed a shocking 324 kilograms (713 lbs) and measured 2.50 meters (8 ft 2 in.) long. Not surprisingly, the giant sea bass can be dangerous to humans.

Prior to the 1950's, this species of bony fish was very common to the near shore waters of Southern California. Due to over-fishing, their population was reduced to critically low levels. In 1982, both commercial and sport fishing of Giant Black Sea Bass was banned in California waters.
—*Channel Islands National Park*

Upper left: Observing one of the remaining giant sea bass at a public aquarium.
Below: Close-up of a giant sea bass head.

Threat	8/10
Uniqueness	6/10
Human responsability	9.5/10
Hope	8/10
Symbolism	5.5/10
Average score	7.4/10

An incredible nineteen out of twenty-one species of albatross are threatened with extinction. The Amsterdam albatross is considered critically endangered by the IUCN, with an estimated 130 birds living.

This is a huge bird, with a wingspan between 280-340 centimeters (110-130 in.). It breeds on Amsterdam Island in the Indian Ocean's French Southern Territories. Its whereabouts outside breeding season are little known, although there have been unconfirmed sightings in Australia and New Zealand.

Threats to this bird's survival are disease, decreased habitat due to cattle grazing, human interference, and feral cats, a newly introduced predator. Commercial fishing equipment also poses a danger to the Amsterdam albatross's fragile status, as the bird becomes caught on hooks and drowns or starves.

Left: The Indian Ocean and the remote Amsterdam Island.
Above: A male Amsterdam Aabatross feeding chick.

"100,000 albatrosses die each year on fishing hooks. They are being killed in such vast numbers that they can't breed fast enough to keep up. This is putting them in real danger of extinction."
—*BirdLife International*

Threat	7/10
Uniqueness	8/10
Human responsability	5/10
Hope	7.5/10
Symbolism	9.5/10
Average score	7.4/10

The akekee is endemic to the island of Kaua'I, Hawaii, where it thrives in the higher elevations. The IUCN Red List classifies this bird as critically endangered, as it has undergone a dramatic population decline in the last ten years.

Human encroachment into the akekee habitat is largely responsible for its fragile status, as is the relatively new presence of disease-carrying mosquitoes. Even a slight change in temperature can affect the health and status of these delicate birds. They are also vulnerable to rats and other non-native birds that have been introduced to the island.

To help save the akekee, the Alaka'i Wilderness Preserve was created; some protection is also offered in the Koke'e State Park. It is too early to know if the bird will be able to adapt to an increased human presence, but with the introduction of conservation programs, it is hoped that they will rebound.

Left: The akekee. According to the photographer, the bird is hard to see because its because it spends it time on top of the canopy, picking insects out of Ohia buds with its slightly crossed bill.
Above: A scenic view of the lush Kalalau Valley in Waimea Canyon State Park, the remote and isolated natural habitat of the akekee.

Threat	9/10
Uniqueness	7/10
Human responsability	7/10
Hope	7.5/10
Symbolism	6/10
Average score	7.3/10

The kakapo is a nocturnal parrot native to New Zealand; its name literally means "night parrot" in the Māori language. It is the world's only flightless parrot. Although numbers appear to be increasing, in 2009 the total population was estimated to be a meager 125 individuals. They are evaluated as critically endangered on the IUCN Red List.

The kakapo is the heaviest parrot in the world. Because this herbivore evolved on islands that did not have mammals, there was no biological need to fly to escape predators and its wings became redundant. In a reversal of Mother Nature's usual presentation, males put themselves on display while females select their breeding partner. Males are not involved in raising the young.

Historically, Māori tribes kept kakapos as pets and hunted them for meat. The bird's skin and feathers were used for clothing; one cape would typically require about 11,000 feathers. With the arrival of Polynesian and, later, European settlers, new predators were introduced, and rats, cats, and weasels all but wiped out the kakapo.

Conservation efforts began over 100 years ago, in about 1890, when birds were relocated to Fiordland. This group, and others relocated in other conservation attempts, eventually petered out. The introduction of the Kakapo Recovery Plan in the 1980s was the key to saving the bird: remaining populations were moved to two predator-free islands, Codfish (Whenua Hou) and Anchor Island. Today, there is hope for the kakapo because of conservation efforts and also because of the bird's longevity in favorable conditions. It can live up to 90 years of age!

"This is great news—we've still got a long, long road ahead before the kakapo's future is secure but it's a huge milestone for one of the country's favourite birds."
—New Zealand's Conservation Minister Tim Groser, commenting the news of the one hundredth kakapo, March 2009

Threat	9/10
Uniqueness	7/10
Human responsability	7/10
Hope	7.5/10
Symbolism	6/10
Average score	7.3/10

Above: The kakapo, the heaviest parrot in the world, has a life expectancy of 90 years.

This flightless yellow-eyed penguin always seems dressed for cocktails. A native to New Zealand, the penguin is featured on the back of that country's five-dollar bill. There are fewer than 2,000 left in the wild, which has led to an IUCN Red List classification as an endangered species.

This penguin gets its name from the yellow band that runs around its head. Its average weight is seven to eight kilograms (15-18 lbs). It breeds in forested or scrub areas.

The decline of its habitat is a principal cause for scarcity. Another danger faced by the penguins, especially on the South Island, is cats, who attack and kill young penguins. Sea lions also kill between twenty to thirty birds annually. Increases in the occurrence of disease as well as higher water temperatures also contribute to the decline of the population. Data shows that a rise in eco-tourism negatively affects the weight and survival rates of the bird. It is hoped that creating protected lands and territories for the yellow-eyed penguin will increase its numbers.

"It was in 1987 that Dunedin conservationists formed the Yellow-eyed Penguin Trust with the aim of saving the penguin by restoring coastal forest and controlling predators."
—Yellow-eyed Penguin Trust

Above: Molting yellow-eyed penguin (Megadyptes antipodes) at Bushy Beach, Oamaru, New Zealand.
Right: The yellow-eyed penguin is fairly large, averaging 75 cm (30 in) long and weighing about 6.3 kg (14 lbs).

Threat	7.5/10
Uniqueness	7/10
Human responsability	6.5/10
Hope	7/10
Symbolism	8.5/10
Average score	7.3/10

This small felid is about the size of an average house cat. It is extremely rare; in fact, prior to 1998, the only evidence of its existence was two photographs. Unfortunately, few conservation dollars are spent on the Andean mountain cat, which numbers fewer than 2,500 in the wild. The IUCN Red List evaluates it as endangered.

This wild cat lives high above the tree line in the snowy mountain ranges of the Andes in Peru, Bolivia, Chili, and Argentina. It is considered a sacred animal to some indigenous tribes, which results in it being actively hunted for ceremonial purposes or because of local superstition. It is believed that their preferred food source is the mountain chinchilla; since the mountain chinchilla was hunted to near extinction during the fur trade, it is believed that this caused a major drop in the cat population.

Further threats to the species come in the form of habitat loss due to mining and, to a lesser extent, cattle grazing. As farmers move their cattle to higher ground in search of adequate grazing pastures, the cat's territory diminishes. Also, farmers consider the Andean cat a predator to their domestic animals and sometimes kill them.

The Andean Cat Alliance and the Andean Cat Conservation Action Plan were formed to ensure the cat's protection. These networks of researchers are dedicated to observing and recording information and educating local people about its importance. The CITES Appendix I has placed full protection on the species, although enforcement is difficult and unreliable.

Above: The Andean mountain cat is about 60 cm (24 in) long, its tail measures 42 cm (17 in) it weighs 5.5 kg (12 lbs).
Upper right: Trees and fields give way to towering peaks in the Peruvian Andes, the natural habitat of the Andean mountain cat.

Threat	8/10
Uniqueness	6/10
Human responsability	8/10
Hope	6/10
Symbolism	8.5/10
Average score	7.3/10

There are forty-five known subspecies of flying squirrel. Of them, six are critically endangered, four are vulnerable, and four are near-threatened. Although these squirrels are found in different regions throughout the world, the threats they face are similar. The critically endangered species are: the smoky, Namdampha, Sumatran, Mentawi, Sipora, and Temminck's flying squirrels.

Flying squirrels have muscular membranes that extend from their sides to their front limbs and hind legs. This membrane allows the animal to glide through the air with surprising agility and control. They can steer and manage speed by adjusting the tension of this membrane. Flying squirrels require forested territory, although some have adapted to urban environments. They commonly eat seeds, fruits, leaves, and insects. All flying squirrels are nocturnal and use the darkness as protective cover. Their ability to glide from branch to branch is a defense mechanism for avoiding tree-dwelling predators.

Above: A rare northern flying squirrel.

Not all flying squirrels have been studied. Although data varies from one subspecies to the next, most are threatened with severe habitat loss. In these cases, clear-cut logging, transformation of land to agricultural uses, and non-timber industries, such as mining, obliterate squirrel ranges or compromise their food sources.

Some protective measures are in place. The Namdapha flying squirrel, for example, is now part of the protective ranges of the Namdapha National Park in Northeast India. Although this squirrel lives within park territory, human encroachment still threatens its survival. Also, the park lacks the resources necessary to fully enforce species-protection regulations.

Threat	7/10
Uniqueness	9/10
Human responsability	7/10
Hope	7/10
Symbolism	6/10
Average score	7.2/10

"Squirrel teaches us that if you don't succeed at your task immediately, and you keep trying, you can do just about anything!"
—The Seneca Nation about flying squirrel

Opposite page: Detail of the eye of Indian gharial. **Left:** The gharial is one of the longest of all living crocodilians. They average 5 m (16.5 feet) long, but there have been reports of individuals over 6.5 m (21.5 ft) long.

as it suffers from overly dry conditions created by the redirection of water systems. Another issue facing the gharial is the trade of adult male body parts for use in traditional medicine.

S eemingly straight from the age of the dinosaur, the gharial is a critically endangered species native to the North-Indian continent. Some studies indicate that the gharial has experienced a 98 percent drop in its population over the last sixty years. There are fewer than twenty adult males left in the wild.

These are the longest of all living crocodile-like species; adults can grow to about twenty feet and weigh up to 2,200 pounds. Despite their size, they are not ferocious or man-eating; the gharial feeds on small fish with its long, narrow snout-like mouth. They are excellent swimmers, and must push themselves along the ground when on land.

Sadly, this reptile is often killed by fishermen to protect their fish stocks or becomes entangled in fishing nets. Its nests are pillaged by certain tribes who savor its eggs; it was reported that entire nest sites were raided and emptied every year from 2001 to 2005. Wildlife wardens now guard the nests. The damming of rivers in gharial territory has also had a serious impact on the species,

When some conservation efforts began in the 1970s, areas such as Nepal saw a stabilization of populations. There is hope that captive breeding and reintroduction programs will be successful.

"The Indian gharial faces a threat both from fishing and illegal activities like sand-mining that have destroyed its nesting areas."
—Sandeep Behra, head of the WWF's gharial conservation program

"The gharial could be the canary in the coalmine. They are telling us something very important - that our rivers are dying, and that could mean us dying next."
—Herpetologist Rom Whitaker

Threat	7/10
Uniqueness	9/10
Human responsability	6/10
Hope	7.5/10
Symbolism	6.5/10
Average score	7.2/10

Patrick Bonneville: This animal is protected but its natural habitat is not. And if we lose the habitat, we lose the species. Fortunately, its tourist-appeal means the future of this Japanese wildcat is pretty much secured.

An important conservation symbol for Japan, this recently discovered wildcat was first understood to be a distinct species in 1965 and was declared a national Japanese treasure in 1977. There are an estimated 100 individuals left on the island of Iriomote, leading the IUCN to list the species as critically endangered.

About the size of a domestic cat, it is a solitary animal that hunts both day and night for the small mammals, birds, and reptiles that compose its diet. It was believed in the past to be a subspecies of the leopard, but biologists now agree that it is a species on its own; indeed, it has changed very little from its prehistoric form.

Despite conservation efforts from local and national governments, the Iriomote wildcat's habitat has diminished in the past few decades. Unfortunately, these cats prefer to roam the forest edges, coasts, and lowlands that lie principally outside the national park that was intended to protect them.

Two important elements might help the species to survive. Its relatively recent discovery aroused a great deal of curiosity and has made the cat something of a tourist attraction. This ensures its value to the Japanese government. Secondly, with a life span of twelve to sixteen years and a gestation period of sixty days, added to the fact that the kittens are independent at only three months old, the population has the potential to increase relatively quickly in the future.

"At this time, there are no known Iriomote cats in captivity, and they have seldom been kept, making them one of the least known cats as far as captive care."
—The Feline Conservation Federation

Above: A stuffed Iriomote wildcat. Live specimens are seldom seen and it is one of the last wild cats in the world.

Threat	8/10
Uniqueness	7/10
Human responsability	7/10
Hope	6/10
Symbolism	8/10
Average score	7.2/10

Although the wolf is protected under Ethiopia's Wildlife Conservation Regulations, which was created in 1974, there is a lack of cooperation from the Ethiopian government to establish captive populations that could regulate breeding and genetic purity. Other programs currently in place include a dog vaccination campaign, a sterilization program for both dogs and hybrid wolves, a vaccination campaign specifically for the wolf population against rabies, and education programs aimed at communities and schools. There has also been increased funding for patrolling and maintaining the wolf's habitat and the establishment of a committee within Ethiopia to analyze data, organize conservation efforts, and monitor the strength and weaknesses of wolf packs.

The Ethiopian wolf is also known as the Simien or Abyssinian wolf; sometimes it is called a fox. The IUCN Red List evaluates it as endangered.

This long-legged wolf's natural habitat is increasingly scarce; it is currently found in seven small isolated mountain ranges in Ethiopia. Although the wolves are social by nature, they are forced to live in unnaturally large colonies. This could have a negative impact on rodent populations and vegetation growth. Close communities of wolves also spread diseases, especially rabies.

Land conversion for farming and manufacturing continues to be a major threat to the Ethiopian wolf. Domestic livestock rob the wolf's grazing ranges, while commercial farms continue to push further into its territories; this leads to the threat of increased human interaction. Hybridization with domestic dogs has also been detected, resulting in species gene deterioration.

"Rabies is the most dangeous and widespread disease to affect Ethiopian wolves, and is the main cause of mortality in Bale."
—The Ethiopian Wolf Conservation Programme

Threat	7/10
Uniqueness	5/10
Human responsability	9/10
Hope	7.5/10
Symbolism	7.5/10
Average score	7.2/10

The fossa is endemic to Madagascar, where it is the largest carnivorous mammal. Its population has diminished by more than 30 percent over the past three generations (about twenty-one years) and the trend is continuing. According to the IUCN Red List, the fossa is vulnerable to extinction, and conservationists are unsure if the current population size of 2,500 is viable.

This solitary animal is both arboreal and terrestrial and can live above the tree line. Its diet includes lemurs and small forest rodents and reptiles. Closely related to the mongoose, the cat-like fossa has remarkable climbing and jumping abilities.

Left: The fossa is a carnivore that hunts small to medium sized animals. It favorite meal is lemur, another endangered species of Madagascar.
Above: Wild fossa running away from cameras in a Madagascar national park.

Threat	7/10
Uniqueness	8.5/10
Human responsability	7.5/10
Hope	5.5/10
Symbolism	7.5/10
Average score	7.2/10

Since Madagascar suffers from deforestation, fossa groups are isolated from each other, across swathes of destroyed habitat. This affects breeding patterns. Widespread hunting and persecution are other causes for the animal's fragile status. Local residents sometimes consider this mammal a pest to be killed, since it enjoys feeding on domestic fowl. While the fossa has no natural predators, it is occasionally a victim of feral dog packs. Human beings also are a direct threat, as some appear to hunt the fossa with the sole goal of eradicating the species. Others hunt the fossa for medicinal purposes.

The fossa is protected in many regions of Madagascar and is listed in Appendix II of the CITES. Conservation efforts include a successful breeding program, the protection of habitat ranges, and education programs. These will be facilitated by the regulation of laws between various levels of government.

"The worst case scenario for the fossa is a similar worst case scenario for Madagascar, with a few other variables thrown in. Madagascar has about eight percent of its original standing forests left. That's bad. The majority of those forests have been lost in the last fifty years. That's worse. It's a recent trend and it's fast, it's going quickly at the to the tune of three to six percent per year."
—Dr. Luke Dollar, Duke University's Nicholas School of the Environment

64 - FLORIDA PANTHER

There is debate as to the uniqueness of the Florida panther. Experts are uncertain if a reclassification is necessary to group this wild cat into the cougar family. DNA studies seem to suggest that it is not a subspecies. Nevetheless, the population of the wild cat in Florida is seriously threatened.

The Florida panther lives in the eastern United States and can be found in Big Cypress National Preserve, Everglades National Park, and the Florida Panther National Wildlife Refuge. Because of its classification issues, the IUCN's Red List only lists the subpopulation in Florida as an Endangered species. Other cougar populations are not included in this particular listing. The current population is estimated to between 70 and 80. Hope is that through reintroduction of puma from other regions, this population will increase.

They are threatened through loss of habitat and fragmentation of groups. They also suffer from poaching of their wild prey base. The Florida Panther does not seem to be hunted and the species is well protected in Florida.

Lower left: Close-up of a wild Florida panther.
Above: Captive Florida panther sleeping behind bars.
Right: Road sign in Florida Everglades National Park.

"Because of habitat loss, now compounded by climate disruption, fewer than 100 of the magnificent cats remain in Florida's Everglades, the animal's only home."
—Sierra Club

Threat	10/10
Uniqueness	6/10
Human responsability	7/10
Hope	7.5/10
Symbolism	5/10
Average score	7.1/10

The Visayan warty pig of the central Philippines is considered critically endangered. Their numbers are perilously decreasing because of habitat loss, food shortage, hunting, and hybridization.

The warty pig now lives on only two of central Philippine's Visayan islands, although historically, it may have been found on many others. In the past the animal roamed regions of varying altitudes, but changes to its natural habitat have pushed it to mainly reside in dense grasslands at an altitude of about 800 meters. Although the species is robust and can survive in less than ideal conditions, extreme hunting, habitat and food loss, as well as inter-species breading are leading this animal to the brink of extinction.

Interaction with humans has been particularly devastating to the pig, which is often viewed as a pest when impinging on farmland. Hunters also target the wild warty pig, whose meat has a market value about double that of regular pork.

The Philippine government now fully protects the pig, however conservation laws are difficult to enforce because of a lack of resources. Experts are hopeful that the pig will thrive in some small regions that have been declared protected areas. The Visayan Warty Pig Conservation Programme, a partnership between the Philippines and the Zoological Society of San Diego, was created in 1992 in an effort to educate residents and protect the animal.

"The Association of Zoos and Aquariums (AZA) sent out an urgent nationwide appeal for zoos to implement emergency breeding programs. The Oregon Zoo joins the San Diego Zoo, St. Louis Zoo and the Los Angeles Zoo to become the fourth in the nation to help in the recovery effort."
—The Oregon Zoo

Above: A captive visayan warty pig. In Europe, the species can be seen in only 5 zoos: Rotterdam Zoo, Poznan Zoo, Chester Zoo, Edinburgh Zoo, and Newquay Zoo.

Threat	10/10
Uniqueness	6/10
Human responsability	7/10
Hope	7.5/10
Symbolism	5/10
Average score	7.1/10

Left: Baby seal on beach in Galápagos.

The sealing fishery nearly extinguished the seal in the early twentieth century, although the population bounced back. Today's seal is vulnerable to environmental changes: El Niño had a devastating impact on the population during the 1982-1983 season, when a high pup mortality was recorded because of a lack of food sources. A further threat comes from ocean pollution, which deteriorates the seal's thick pelage, which in turn reduces its ability to maintain a normal body temperature. There are also recorded events of the seal being trapped in local fishing nets, a trend that appears to be on the increase.

The outlook for the Galápagos fur seal is tenuous: despite its relatively high numbers, it remains vulnerable because of restricted distribution. A single wave of disease could decimate the colonies, as could another severe El Niño season.

The Galápagos fur seal appears on the IUCN Red List as an endangered species because of its limited range, unstable numbers, and a population reduction of over 50 percent in the past thirty years. Its current population is estimated between 15,000 and 20,000 and is expected to continue to drop.

These non-migratory seals are the smallest of all pinnipeds, or fin-footed mammals. They live in colonies on the rocky shores of the Galápagos islands, where they spend about 70 percent of their time on land—more than the average seal. They enter the water only to feed. Females claim a territory in which to raise their young for a period of up to two years. Galápagos fur seals can live up to twenty years.

Threat	7/10
Uniqueness	7/10
Human responsability	7.5/10
Hope	6/10
Symbolism	8/10
Average score	7.1/10

"Although 95 percent of the species that were there when humans first arrived still exist in the Galapagos, IUCN - the World Conservation Union lists dozens on its "red list" of threatened species. These include the Galapagos hawk and the Galapagos fur seal, along with 57 species of Bulimulus snails. On some of the ten larger islands, alien species have already led to the extinction of native species."
—*The Galapagos Conservation Trust*

Darwin's fox, or Darwin's zorro, is a small fox native to Chiloé Island and Nahuelbuta National Park in mainland Chile. Its population in the two regions where it is found amounts to fewer than 250 mature individuals. It is considered critically endangered by the IUCN.

Charles Darwin first studied this forest dweller in 1834. It was initially assumed to be a subspecies of the South American gray fox, but genetic analysis proved its individuality. Darwin's fox does not interbreed with other fox species. Long believed to be limited to the island of Chiloé, in 1990 a small population was found on mainland Chile. Chiloé Island broke apart from the mainland about fifteen thousand years ago, isolating Darwin's Fox from other fox populations. Ninety percent of the foxes are found on the island.

The national park population is threatened by dogs that bring disease or attack the fox. Farmers encourage dogs to pursue foxes in order to protect their herds and crops. The fox population on the island is exposed to poaching and its habitat is threatened by logging. There have been reports of foxes being kept illegally as pets.

Above: A rare photo of a wild Darwin's fox, Ahuenco, Chiloe Island, Chile.

Darwin's fox has been protected by Chilean law since 1929, although enforcement is not sufficient to stop continued poaching. Conservationists hope that the fox has found remote regions to inhabit and that such isolated populations can thrive.

"A fox (Canis fulvipes), of a kind said to be peculiar to the island and very rare in it, and which is a new species, was sitting on the rocks. He was so intently absorbed in watching the work of the officers that I was able, by quietly walking up behind, to knock him on the head with a geological hammer. This fox, more curious or more scientific, but less wise than the generality of his brethren is now mounted in the museum of the Zoological Society."
—Charles Darwin, excerpt from "Naturalist's Voyage Round the World"

Threat	8/10
Uniqueness	5/10
Human responsability	7/10
Hope	8/10
Symbolism	7/10
Average score	7.0/10

The walia ibex is a species of goat that is threatened by habitat loss, poaching, and war. The world's only population of this goat lives in the Simien Mountains of Ethiopia, where there are about 400 individuals. The IUCN evaluates the walia ibex as endangered.

The ibex lives in a national park, where its only known predator is the hyena. Numbers have slowly increased over the past few years, however the ibex is still threatened by human encroachment. During the past two decades of the region's war and instability, people have settled within or close to park boundaries—there are an estimated 30,000 people just outside the national park boundaries.

The walia ibex is protected by both national and regional laws, but its preference for remote regions and a lack of resources for conservation efforts in Ethiopia make it difficult to enforce anti-poaching laws. Occasionally, walia ibex also roam away from protected areas to feed on cultivated crops, which sometimes leads to their being killed by farmers.

Ethiopia has placed the walia ibex under a no-hunt law, although a special permit for hunting can be had for scientific purposes. Saving this goat is the emblem for the Ethiopian Wildlife Conservation Organization and the Ethiopian Wildlife and Natural History Society.

Lower left: The Ethiopian region of the Simien Mountains is the only natural habitat of the Walia Ibex. The animal weighs up to 125 kg (280 lb).
Above: A Walia Ibex and a Gelada Baboon in the Simien Mountains, Ethiopia.

Threat	8/10
Uniqueness	7/10
Human responsability	6.5/10
Hope	6/10
Symbolism	7/10
Average score	6.9/10

The yellow-tailed woolly is a rare monkey endemic to Peru. With an estimated 250 left in the wild, it has a ranking of critically endangered on the IUCN Red List. Its numbers have dwindled because of habitat loss, sport hunting, bushmeat hunting, and the pet trade.

The yellow-tailed woolly remained isolated high in the Peruvian Andes until the 1950s, when colonization projects, road-building, and urban sprawl brought drastic change to the monkey's territory. It was not long before mining and logging arrived.

Several protected regions have been created, including Abiseo National Park, Bosque de Protección Alto Mayo and the Reserved Zone Cordillera de Colán. A fourth zone, the Asociación Peruana para la Conservación de la Naturaleza has not yet been formally accepted.

In order to ensure the long-term survival of this delicate monkey, conservation efforts must be initiated and rigorously enforced. Education with local tribes will need to play an important part of these efforts, but so too will revised urban planning and industrial exploitation of the territories.

Left: The yellow-tailed wooly lives only in the montane cloud forests of the Peruvian Andes at elevations of 1700 - 2500 m (5600' - 8200').
Right: Woolly monkeys are known for their fur that protects them from the cold.

"Clearing the forest for agriculture continues at an alarming rate, even in the Protected Forest of Alto Mayo (BPAM). It has been estimated that between 2,300 and 2,500 ha of forest have been destroyed in BPAM (ParksWatch, Peru). The forest of the BPAM is now considerably fragmented, a result of lack of enforcement and a substantial human population living in the Protected Forest itself."
—IUCN/SSC Primate Specialist Group

Threat	7/10
Uniqueness	8/10
Human responsability	7/10
Hope	6/10
Symbolism	6.5/10
Average score	6.9/10

The fishing cat is distributed widely throughout the wetlands of Southeast Asia. It is now extinct in China, Malaysia and Pakistan as well as certain regions of India, and groups elsewhere in Asia have declined steadily for about 18 years. It is considered endangered by the IUCN.

Threats to the cat include human activity, including encroachment, agriculture, pollution, hunting, fishing, and forestry. The clearance of coastal mangroves and the depletion of fish stocks mean the fishing cat's habitat and food sources are dwindling. Incidental poisoning and accidental snaring of fishing cats have also contributed to their decline.

Left: Fishing cats have grey and brown fur with a mix of stripes and spots. Excellent swimmers, they live near rivers, streams and swamps, hence their name "fishing cat".
Above: The fishing cat has a flat-nosed face.

Experts expect the trend to continue unless radical adjustments in human behavior and important progress in conservation efforts are initiated. Very few sightings of the cat have been noted in Thailand in recent years and no sightings in Viet Nam have been recorded since 1995. The situation is so dire in Indonesia that its status could be changed to critically endangered. In countries where the cat remains, populations are widely dispersed and conditions for survival are doubtful.

The fishing cat is included in the CITES Appendix II. It also benefits from legal protection from hunting throughout much of its habitat range, although enforcement of law is difficult to manage and funding is scarce. Without measure to ensure adequate wetland protection, however, the fishing cat faces a grim outlook.

"Fishing cats appear to have a high tolerance for human activity and impacts and this increases the overall risk of human-cat conflict."
—The Fishing Cat Research and Conservation Project

Threat	9/10
Uniqueness	6/10
Human responsability	7/10
Hope	6/10
Symbolism	6.5/10
Average score	6.9/10

The Forest owlet was believed to be extinct for 113 years, with its last sighting in 1884. In 1997 it was rediscovered by Pamela Rasmussen and is today considered critically endangered.

This small and stocky owl is found in the forests of central India, where its population numbers about 100. Its territories are threatened by human encroachment, namely from the forest industry, forest fires, and farming. Because of the rarity of sightings of this bird, it is difficult to identify any other threats that might be causing its low numbers. It is believed that pesticides could also be a threat, however more study is required to confirm such an hypothesis.

"One hundred and thirteen years after the last genuine record, the Forest Owlet, Athene blewitti has been rediscovered in the low foothills dry-deciduous forest north of Shahada, Maharashtra, India."
—Pamela C. Rasmussen and Ben F. King, from the Smithsonian Institution and the American Museum of Natural History, 1998

Above: A very clear image of a forest owlet.
Right: The forest owlet waits, motionless in trees, for its prey.

Threat	8/10
Uniqueness	6/10
Human responsability	8/10
Hope	6/10
Symbolism	6.5/10
Average score	6.9/10

Kemp's Ridley is the smallest of all living sea turtles, and it is also the rarest. In the 1940s, as many as 100,000 females would nest in a single day; today, only 1,000 nesting females exist. The IUCN lists the ridley turtle as critically endangered.

Allegedly named for the Florida fisherman who captured and sent a specimen of this small species to Harvard in 1906 for study, Kemp turtles lay their eggs in the Mexican state of Tamaulipas. They prefer to live in warm waters, although some have been sighted as far north as New Jersey. It is believed that this turtle plays a vital role in coastal and open ocean ecosystems, where they feed on invertebrates and aid the oceans in population control.

Various threats include exploitation of eggs, slaughter for meat, bycatch from the shrimp industry, and ocean pollution. Eggs are a quick meal for coyotes, skunks, and raccoons, while many humans believe turtle eggs to be aphrodisiac. Oil spills, pollution, and pesticide run-off also affect the turtle's health. This turtle's biggest threat, however, is fishing nets. Some shrimp trawlers are now equipped with turtle excluder devices that help detect turtle groups.

The fate of the Kemp's Ridley turtle has been monitored since the 1970s and conservation efforts by both the USA and Mexico have resulted in a slight increase in population. The nesting beach of Rancho Nuevo in Mexico was declared a national reserve, and beach patrolling has been increased to curb egg thieving.

"Since the principal nesting beach is in Mexico, the continued, long-term cooperation of two nations is necessary to recover the species. A joint United States-Mexican management program is underway which includes nesting beach protection and incubation of eggs."
—Texas Parks and Wildlife Department

Above: Female turtles return to beaches in northern Mexico and Texas to lay their eggs. The Mexican-U. S. border is the only region where the Kemp's Ridley offspring see daylight. It is the rarest sea turtle in the world.

Threat	8/10
Uniqueness	5/10
Human responsability	9/10
Hope	7/10
Symbolism	5/10
Average score	6.8/10

Left: A fruit bat hanging from a tree near Melbourne, Australia.

(3.3 pounds). Most species live in Asia, on the Indian subcontinent, Indonesia, Australia, on some islands off the east coast of Africa, and on some isolated Atlantic and Pacific islands. Their diet consists of nectar, pollen, and fruit.

They have many predators, mostly birds of prey and snakes. Humans are the worst of their predators, however, since flying foxes are a ready source of meat. Over-harvesting has resulted in dramatic declines in their populations. Action has been taken to change the trend toward extinction: in 1989, all species of flying fox were placed on the CITES Appendix II of threatened species, and at least seven of them were placed on Appendix I, for endangered species. Unfortunately, illegal hunting continues.

Patrick Bonneville: With the disappearance of the flying fox, humanity is responsible for the disappearance of one of the oldest creatures on earth.

Flying foxes, also known as pteropus or fruit bats, are the largest bats in the world. The IUCN lists seventy-two species of flying fox, of which seventeen are listed as critically endangered or endangered and four as extinct. For most of the remaining species, there is not enough data to accurately establish their vulnerability to extinction.

The largest of these megabats are aerodynamically efficient flying creatures with a wingspan of up to 1.83 meters (six feet) and a weight of only 1.5 kg

"Fruit bats play a vital role in the ecology of the rainforests where they live. Old world fruit bats eat the fruit, nectar or flowers of more than 300 plant species, and these plants rely on the bats for seed dispersal and pollination."
—Scott Heinrichs, founder Flying Fox Conservation Fund

Threat	8/10
Uniqueness	8/10
Human responsability	6/10
Hope	7/10
Symbolism	5/10
Average score	6.8/10

The Madagascar serpent-eagle is a bird of prey that was previously thought to be extinct, with a last confirmed sighting in 1950. Subsequent sightings later led the Peregrine Fund to officially list the bird as rediscovered in 1993. With a current population of between 250 and 300 individuals, the IUCN considers the Madagascar serpent-eagle endangered.

This hooked-beak raptor lives in Madagascar, a unique island whose wildlife remained isolated for about 160 million years; 85 percent of the island's flora cannot be found anywhere else on the planet.

Recently, specimens have been spotted outside the bird's traditional territory, raising hopes that it is extending its range—likely in search of food and safe shelter. Nevertheless, degradation of this bird's specialized habitat means its forecast for ongoing survival is tenuous.

Lower Left: The Madasgascar serpent-eagle cousin, an Asian serpent-eagle with wide-open wings.
Above: The lush green mountains of Madagascar, the natural habitat of the very rare Madagascar serpent-eagle.

"It was about 5:30 in the morning, and I was out learning the trails in an area I was assigned to survey. I heard this vocalization I hadn't heard before, and then I saw this big raptor fly. Earlier, I had seen a hawk that is very easily confused with the eagle, but I was 98 percent confident that this was a serpent eagle."
—scientist Russell Thorstrom who rediscovered the Madagascar Serpent-eagle in 1993

Threat	7/10
Uniqueness	7.5/10
Human responsability	7.5/10
Hope	8/10
Symbolism	4/10
Average score	6.8/10

Patrick Bonneville: This rare rabbit looks like no other. I contacted many specialized organizations in order to find just one photo, and despite their goodwill, the photo was impossible to find. That says it all. This rabbit either knows very well how to avoid human contact or else it just might be gone forever.

Above: The only recent image available of a Sumatran rabbit. It still exists, but the animal might become extinct very soon.

This naturally elusive animal offers up little information for conservationists; its nocturnal nature and presumed small population mean that it is difficult to study. Listed as critically endangered in 1996 by IUCN experts, its actual numbers are unknown. It is endemic to the island of Sumatra in Indonesia, where it was last photographed by a camera trap in 2007. It is known to live in the west-central and southwestern part of Sumatra and in the Gunung Leuser National Park.

As with many other of Indonesia's species, the main threat to this rabbit's survival is the clearing of mountain forest for agriculture. Coffee, tea, and cocoa plantations have quickly taken over large parts of forests in the region.

In order to establish a conservation plan, IUCN and local specialists will need to localize the specific geographic area where the small rabbit population lives. Many hope they will find Sumatran striped rabbits in an already protected area such as the Gumai Pasemah Wildlife Reserve, the Kerinci Seblat National Park, or the Bukit Barisan National Park.

"This shy nocturnal animal is so rare and well hidden that local people do not have a name for it in their own language and many do not even realise that it exists."
—The EDGE of Existence programme

"This rabbit is so poorly known that any proof of its continued existence at all is great news, and confirms the conservation importance of Sumatra's forests."
—Colin Poole, director of the Wildlife Conservation Society's Asia Program.

Threat	9/10
Uniqueness	5/10
Human responsability	7/10
Hope	7/10
Symbolism	6/10
Average score	6.8/10

The Fiji crested iguana is a critically endangered species of iguana native to certain Fiji islands. The species is thought to have evolved from an iguana species which travelled from South America 13 million years ago. The spectacular animal became well known after a few appearances in the movie *Blue Lagoon*.

It is almost completely green, and is distinguishable from other iguanas living in the Fiji islands by its three white bands. It measures 76 cm (30 in) and it weighs 300 grams (0.66 lb). Once present on fourteen islands, the species can now be found only on three. The island Yadua Taba has the highest concentration with 6,000 individuals. It is the only protected group of iguanas in the world.

While the species was listed as vulnerable by IUCN's Red List in 1996, it is now considered critically endangered With only one important population left in the world, the species has became extremely vulnerable to illness and natural disaster.

Fortunately, the island of Yadua Taba is well protected. It is home to the best protected dry Pacific forests in the world, maily because of the presence of the Fiji Crested Iguana. Introduction of new species and fires are strictly prohibited in the region. As long as Yadua Taba is saved and protected, the Fiji crested iguana will survive.

"The long-term plan is to transfer second generation iguanas to zoos in Australasia to establish an insurance population and further safeguard against a complete collapse of the species in the wild."
—*Dr. Peter Harlow, international expert on Fijian Crested Iguanas*

Threat	7.5/10
Uniqueness	5/10
Human responsability	8.5/10
Hope	7.5/10
Symbolism	5.5/10
Average score	6.8/10

Left: In Fiji, the crested iguana is known as locally known as *vokai* or *saumuri*. Iguanas are important in Fiji folklore. Most Fijians, however, are afraid of the creature because it reacts strongly in the presence of humans or other threat.

Patrick Bonneville: One more gibbon. They all seem to be disappearing.

This is probably the last decade for the silvery gibbon. The Indonesian species counts less than 2,000 individuals alive in the wild on the island of Java. It lives in Java's western provinces, in Banten and West Java. Subpopulations are also found in central Java. The wild population is decreasing.

While the animal habitat is being destroyed, many residents in Indonesia have taken silvery gibbons as personal pets. The illegal trade of the silvery gibbon is an important one. People especially like the young ones. Adult gibbons are often slaughtered so that their babies can be sold as pets.

According to the IUCN, the habitat loss continues due to deforestation but at a much slower rate than in the past. Despite the fact that many zoos house the species, especially in Indonesia, captive breeding programs do not seem successful. The female is known to give birth only every 3 or 4 years in the wild. Survival and repopulation seems even more difficult for captive individuals. Conservation efforts continue, but education of the local population and enforcement from the local authorities are necessary to save the silvery gibbon.

"The haunting and beautiful call of the female Silvery Gibbon still awakens a few small patches of the misty rainforests of West and Central Java. Unlike most gibbon species, her mate contributes little to the song but watches for intruders during the female's early morning recital. Sadly, the call of the Silvery Gibbon could be silenced forever."
—*The Silvery Gibbon Project*

Left: A rare silvery gibbon.
Right: Only a few zoos outside Indonesia have silvery gibbons. Even the captive population is endangered.

Threat	8/10
Uniqueness	4/10
Human responsability	7/10
Hope	8/10
Symbolism	7/10
Average score	6.8/10

The major threats to the red panda are habitat loss, fragmentation, poaching and inbreeding. As forests are felled, populations become separated and small pockets inbreed as a result. Illegal hunting poses a serious threat to the species.

The red panda is protected under Appendix I of CITES and Schedule I of the Indian Wild Life Protection Act. Similar protect laws exist in Bhutan, China, Nepal and Myanmar. Captive breeding programs show promising hope. Programs exist in various parts of the world including North America (Species Survival Plan – SSP), Europe (European Endangered Species Programme - EEP), Australia, India, Japan and China. Both the International Studbook (Rotterdam Zoo in the Netherlands) and the International Red Panda Management Group coordinate all breeding programs.

The red panda is also known under the names of lesser panda, red cat-bear and Tolai hair. According to the IUCN's Red List, the red panda is vulnerable due to its low population count and continuing decline in population over three generations (about thirty years). There is an estimated population of about 10,000 mature individuals and this number declines at a rate of 10% per generation.

The assumed range includes Nepal, India, Bhutan, Myanmar, and southern China. There have been reports of the red panda in Lao People's Democratic Republic as well. The red panda prefers temperate forests with bamboo thickets. The red panda's territory overlaps with the Giant Panda's territory through certain regions of China. Although the species is not as threatened as its very distant cousin the giant panda, both species rely on bamboo forests for their continued survival and as such, both species are victim to deforestation.

"Rimbick, an Indian village on the perimeter of the park, was once the hub for the international red panda trade. According to locals, 47 red pandas were sold in one year from this village to stock the zoos of the world."
—*Red Panda Network*

Left: Red panda feeding on bamboo leaf.
Upper right: The Red Panda is found mainly in temperate forests in the Himalayas.

Threat	7/10
Uniqueness	8.5/10
Human responsability	5.5/10
Hope	4.5/10
Symbolism	8.5/10
Average score	6.8/10

Patrick Bonneville: This beautiful and colorful bird is like a tiny flying rainbow!

The Gouldian finch is found only in Australia, where it is also called the rainbow finch. According to the IUCN Red List, the bird is endangered because of its small population that continues to decline despite conservation efforts.

British ornithological artist John Gould described the bird in 1844 and named it in honor of his wife. These finches live in the savanna woodlands of northwestern Australia, where they typically stay within a range of about forty square kilometers (15.5 sq. miles). They are social birds who fly in large flocks, but they are shy of humans. With its introduction to other countries, the Gouldian finch species has developed various color mutations, including white.

Above: Gouldian finches' heads may be red, black, or yellow.
Right: The male bird's chest is purple, while the female's is a lighter mauve colour.

Habitat modification from forest fires, the transformation of land for agriculture, and water quality are the main threats to these birds. Conservative numbers place the best-known flock, one that has shown population stability, at about 10,000 mature individuals.

The good news is that conservation efforts so far have slowed the decline of the Gouldian finch. The Mornington Wildlife Sanctuary in Kimberley is preparing an action plan that will help the species make a full recovery. They will address issues such as the presence of cattle and other livestock trampling the vegetation that is essential for the finches, and whose presence also alters conditions around the waterholes used by the birds. The sanctuary will also address effective fire control, as fire can ravage the grasslands and destroy seeds that the finches feed on.

Threat	9/10
Uniqueness	7/10
Human responsability	7/10
Hope	6.5/10
Symbolism	4/10
Average score	6.7/10

Patrick Bonneville: A small population, heavy illegal hunting, and habitat destruction are the three main ingredients in the recipe for extinction. Right now, the Chacoan peccary is in the soup pot.

This pig-like species is endemic to the Gran Chaco, a hot and arid lowland region of the Río de la Plata basin, where Paraguay, Argentina, and Bolivia meet. The name of the region means "hunting land," which is significant in understanding why the peccary is endangered here. It has been listed as endangered by the IUCN, since the whole population has dropped by half over three generations of reproduction. There are currently estimated to be 3,000 individuals in the wild.

Known locally as tagua, it lives and moves in herds, usually early in the day. This makes it an appealing target for hunters. Chacoan peccaries feed on the cacti commonly found in its range, and rub the prickly spines from a cactus by rolling it on the ground with their snout. Its kidneys and two stomachs are adapted to be able to digest the acidic cacti.

Despite hunting prohibitions in Paraguay and in Argentina, the Chacoan peccary is still heavily hunted for its meat. Increasingly, habitat destruction and disease are affecting their fragile population as well. They do not adapt well to captivity.

Above: Captive Chacoan peccary at the Phoenix Zoo in Arizona.

The Chacoan peccary is included on the CITES Appendix I; however, anti-poaching regulations are not respected or enforced. Even official wildlife havens do not fully protect the peccary from illegal hunting. Reinforcements, especially in the Copo National Park and in Kaa-lya del Gran Chaco National-al Park, must be introduced in order to help conserve this little hoofed animal.

"This is the first new, large, living mammal that has been found since about the turn of the century, when the okapi was found in the jungle of Africa."
—*Dr. Ralph M. Wetzel, who discovered the species in 1972*

Threat	8/10
Uniqueness	7.5/10
Human responsability	7/10
Hope	6/10
Symbolism	5/10
Average score	6.7/10

This species is endemic to the mountains of Vancouver Island, Canada, and is the only marmot found on that island. The IUCN Red List evaluates it as critically endangered, with only thirty-five individuals left in the wild as of 2004. With a rate of decline of more than 80 percent over three generations, chances are high that the Vancouver Island marmot will be extinct within twenty years.

Mukmuk, the "sidekick" to the three official mascots of Vancouver, Canada's 2010 Winter Olympics, is a Vancouver Island marmot. The species is also the conservation emblem for the province of British Colombia. It is a unique species as far as marmots go, in terms of morphology, genetics, behavior, and ecology. It is believed to have rapidly evolved on the island since the last glacial retreat, about 10,000 years ago. Its weight fluctuates significantly, depending on the season: after about long 210 days of hibernation, from late September to late April, the marmot emerges some two or three kilograms (4.5 or 6.5 pounds) lighter than in the fall.

The greatest threat to the survival of the marmots is from the forestry industry. Clearcut logging landscapes are attractive to the animals in the summer, where they find good soil for burrowing and stumps to use as lookouts. But conservationists worry that these swathes of land offer poor conditions for hibernation. The marmots may not, then, make it to more suitable ranges to reproduce with others of their species.

Left: A Vancouver Island marmot enjoys early morning sun in an alpine meadow on Vancouver Island
Above: Canadian Ffag flying from a ferry on its way back from Vancouver Island.

Conservation efforts have been developed that include captive breeding and reintroduction. Because it is one of the world's rarest mammals, efforts to create "genetic lifeboats" were made by the Toronto Zoo, which took up the challenge in 1977, and by the Calgary Zoo and the Mountainview Conservation and the Breeding Centre in Langley, British Columbia. In 2007 the captive breeding programs showed success with sixty pups born, bringing the total in captivity to 162. In 2003, marmots from these locations were released into the wild in hopes of raising the population.

Threat	8/10
Uniqueness	5/10
Human responsability	7/10
Hope	6/10
Symbolism	7.5/10
Average score	6.7/10

This rodent lives in the dry, sandy grasslands of California. The IUCN Red List evaluates it as endangered because of its extremely fragmented range and deteriorating habitat. Current estimates indicate there are about 100 distinct populations, made up of about 100,000 individuals. Once abundant throughout many counties, contemporary sightings have been recorded in five small regions, including in the San Joaquin Valley.

Giant kangaroo rats live in groups and communicate with other members and indicate their territory by drumming their feet on the ground. They are an important link in the food chain; their survival is paramount to the survival of several other species. The rats are vegetarian, preferring roots, seeds and grasses. They are a food source for predators, including foxes, owls, and snakes. The rats also contributes to the re-establishment of grasses by spreading seeds as they dig for roots. They live an average of two to three years.

Their decline is attributed to human activity, especially to habitat change brought about by the petroleum industry, urbanization, and livestock farming. Pesticide and rodenticide use are additional factors. The already fragile giant kangaroo rat is also vulnerable to Mother Nature and her droughts, floods, and fires.

Habitat protection varies according to the region. Since 1980, state and federal government reserves in California have protected the giant kangaroo rat to varying degrees.

Below: The Californian species is the largest of all kangaroo rats, measuring about 15 cm (6 in.) in length, excluding its impressive long tail.
Right: Cultivated farm land in the San Joaquin Valley in California, the only region where the giant kangaroo rat is now found.

Threat	7.5/10
Uniqueness	7.5/10
Human responsability	7/10
Hope	6/10
Symbolism	5/10
Average score	6.6/10

Threat	7/10
Uniqueness	7/10
Human responsability	7.5/10
Hope	6/10
Symbolism	5.5/10
Average score	6.6/10

Patrick Bonneville: When I researched the proboscis monkey, I was stunned by the fascinating and gentle-looking creature. I remembered that I first saw this species as a child in The Adventures of Tintin, in the comic-strip album Flight 714 *published in 1968. I hope this big-nosed monkey does not only survive in my childhood memories.*

Proboscis monkeys live in specific small areas in Brunei and Indonesian Borneo. In the last fifty years, the species has lost between 50 to 80 percent of its population. There are now some 1,000 left in the wild, leading the IUCN to list it as an endangered species.

These monkeys live mostly in coastal lowland forests, such as mangroves and swamps; they stay close to coastal fresh water and rivers where there is a lower concentration of minerals and salt. Males are about double the weight of females, which makes theirs the greatest gender size difference among all the primates. The nose of a male can grow up to seven inches long, and is used to attract females and amplify warning calls.

Because they are relatively sedentary, they are exposed to habitat loss and become easy targets for hunters who use the monkeys for food or sell body parts for use in traditional Chinese medicine. Their habitat has been severely damaged by forest fires in the past two decades; according to IUCN, the 1997-1998 forest fires that occurred in one region are thought to have destroyed a significant portion of the proboscis monkey's habitat. Since then, recovery has been slow.

The proboscis monkey is listed on CITES Appendix I and is officially protected, but these measures are not reinforced by local government. Unfortunately, the species does not do well in captivity because of its diet—the leaves it eats can only be found in its natural habitat.

"On Borneo live some of Nature's most remarkable creations—from the orang-utan to the world's largest flower, and from the proboscis monkey to tropical pitcher plants. For many of these species Borneo is their last stronghold. Once extinguished there, they will be gone forever. And Borneo is changing rapidly."
—Sir Peter Crane , former director of the Royal Botanic Gardens in Kew, London

Opposite page: A wild proboscis monkey in Borneo.
Left: The animal's nose is thought to be used to attract females. It also turns red when the animal feels threatened and becomes agitated.

Found in the western Himalayan hills of Uttaranchal, in north-west India, this bird was already considered rare by the end of the nineteenth century. According to many experts it is now extinct, since no official sightings have occurred since 1876. Unconfirmed sightings, including one recorded around Naini Tal in 2003, give rise to hope that some of these birds are still alive. The IUCN Red List considers the Himalayan quail critically endangered until further field research can confirm or deny its existence.

Left: A common quail. The Himalayan quail has white spots around its eye.
Above: Indian Himalaya near the spring of the Ganges River, the species' natural habitat.

Evidence suggests that prior to 1877, it was a relatively common bird. By the late 1880s, however, it was difficult to find any specimens. Nineteenth-century observers noted that the elusive bird was well hidden in dense grasses on south-facing slopes up to 2,400 meters in altitude. It was believed that they migrated to even higher altitudes for breeding. The quails seemed to congregate in coveys of six to twelve birds and seemed never to fly, unless about to be trampled by observers.

Hunting during the colonial occupation of India is the suspected cause of decline in quail numbers. Another contributor was likely the increase in land exploitation, such as mining for limestone. Illustrations of the bird exist, as well as at least one stuffed specimen, at the National Museum of Natural History in Leiden, the Netherlands. Since there have been only a few well-organized efforts to find the bird, it is hoped that more thorough future surveys will confirm the survival of the Himalayan quail.

Threat	8/10
Uniqueness	6/10
Human responsability	7.5/10
Hope	6/10
Symbolism	5/10
Average score	6.5/10

The Hispaniolan solenodon looks much like a giant shrew, although it is a mammal. It is found only on the island of Hispaniola, home to Haiti and the Dominican Republic. It was first officially discovered in 1833, along with another species of solenodon, now extinct. Because of its nocturnal habits, it was rarely seen and studied by scientists. The IUCN Red List considers it endangered. Since very few can be surveyed, there may be a need to uplist it to critically endangered.

Hispaniolan solenodons are one of the rare venomous mammals; their second lower incisors have a narrow groove through which the animal secretes venomous saliva. When they venture out of their burrow, they move slowly and clumsily, and often trip over their own feet and tumble. They eat anthropods, worms, and snails and have been observed killing and eating a chicken. They use their long snouts to dig or to open logs in search of food. They have been observed as being frequent bathers and seem to drink only when bathing. The animal also has spines that become erect under threat, as well as special glands under its arms and in its groin area that give off an unpleasant, goat-like smell. Even other solenodons are vulnerable to the venom from an attacking solendon.

Historically, the solenodon had very few natural predators on Hispaniola. Once people began introducing non-native mammals, such as the small Asian mongoose, dogs, and cats, in an effort to curb the escalating rat population, the solenodon's population began to decline. Humans have compromised its habitat by transforming natural lands into agricultural land. Also, in Haiti, the animal is hunted as an exotic food item.

In 2008, film crews captured the solenodon in the Dominican Republic; a team of researchers from the Durrell Wildlife Conservation Trust and the Ornithological Society of Hispaniola captured one as well. They were able to record its measurements and analyze its DNA before releasing it back into the wild. The solenodon is protected by law in the Dominican Republic, and there have been suggestions of education programs, surveys, and management efforts for Haiti's Pic Macaya National Park.

Threat	7/10
Uniqueness	7/10
Human responsability	8/10
Hope	6/10
Symbolism	4.5/10
Average score	6.5/10

Right: In relation to its body, the species has an oversized head and long tail.

Left: Individual from the captive breeding program Project Kial, sponsored by the Bridled Nailtail Wallaby Trust

Bridled nailtail wallabys are mostly solitary and nocturnal. Their name comes from a white band that runs down their backs and from a horny spur on the end of their tails. They feed on grasses and herbaceous plants.

The causes of the bridled nailtail's current situation are mainly historical. During colonization, the animal lost most of its habitat to agriculture, and it was also hunted for its fur and as a pest. New species were introduced to the continent as well, putting pressure on the natural resources of the wallaby and introducing new predators. More recently, its habitat has been damaged by natural disasters, including droughts and extraordinarily heavy rains.

Patrick Bonneville: There are no worries about the kangaroo, the national symbol of Australia. The nailtail wallaby, a smaller marsupial, is facing extinction. The number of living individuals is critically low. It might become one more animal we failed to save.

Also known as the flashjack wallaby, the bridled nailtail can still be found in three of Queensland, Australia's national parks: Taunton, Idalia, and Avocet Nature Refuge. Despite conservation efforts, the remaining population—ranging from 200 to 700 depending on the source—still faces danger.

Some successful measures have been taken by the Australian government and the private sector to save this small striped wallaby. Australians authorities have translocated two small groups to the BHP Threatened Species Sanctuary and the Scotia Sanctuary in another region of New South Wales. This is good news. The population is small but stable, and there is hope that numbers will increase in the coming years.

Threat	8/10
Uniqueness	5/10
Human responsability	7.5/10
Hope	6/10
Symbolism	6/10
Average score	6.5/10

"About half of the newly emerged young, weighing only a few hundred grams, are killed by feral cats."
—Bridled Nailtail Wallaby Trust

Once found in twelve American states and two Canadian provinces, there are currently fewer than 250 wild ferrets in Arizona, Montana, South Dakota, and Wyoming. There are eighteen known groups, of which only three have viable populations. The black-footed ferret was once considered extinct in the wild, although thanks to conservation efforts, it has recovered. The IUCN evaluates it as endangered on their Red List.

The black-footed ferret—which is not the same as the domesticated species—is a small carnivorous prairie mammal from the diverse family Mustelidae, which also includes weasels, mink, polecats, martens, otters, and badgers. Their coloring makes for perfect camouflage.

A captive breeding program was initiated in October 1985 in Wyoming, where the Wyoming Game and Fish Department and the United States Fish and Wildlife Service captured eighteen animals between 1985 and 1987. Today, there are six institutions—one federal facility and five zoos—participating in the program, in which more than 6,000 ferrets born in captivity have been reintroduced to the wild in eight states. Its listing in the CITES Appendix I, combined with the breeding programs, engenders hope that the black-footed ferret will make an outstanding recovery and be downlisted.

"Black-footed ferrets are an important part of our natural heritage and ours to restore and protect."
—The Black-footed Ferret Recovery Implementation Team

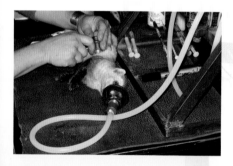

Threat	8/10	
Uniqueness	4/10	
Human responsability	7/10	
Hope	7/10	
Symbolism	6.5/10	
Average score	6.5/10	

Left: Volunteers monitoring health of the black-footed ferret in Wyoming.
Above: Two young Black-footed ferret pups.
Right: Black-footed ferrets are about 45 cm (18 in) long and weigh 1 kg (2 lbs).

The northern hairy-nosed wombat, also known as the yaminon, is found in Australia. It was once common across New South Wales, Victoria, and Queensland, but now only about 115 animals are alive in one range, in the Epping Forest National Park in Queensland. In the early 1980s, the total population had dropped to between thirty and forty. One of the rarest mammals in the world, it is listed as critically endangered on the IUCN Red List.

The northern hairy-nosed wombat underwent an extensive and rapid decline with the introduction of livestock and exotic grasses to their habitat, when competition for grazing with cattle and sheep proved harmful. Predators also played a role—in 2000, about twenty northern hairy-nosed wombats were killed by dingoes.

Above: A native Australian hairy nosed wombat.
Opposite page: Kangaroo and wombat warning signs on the Nullarbor desert highway in Australia.

In what seems to be a first, Xstrata, a $28 billion Swiss global mining company, has sponsored the wombat. Much in the same manner as a company would sponsor any product, in exchange for funding, Xstrata will see its logo and name appear on all sorts of northern hairy-nosed wombat products, from websites to educational materials and uniforms worn by wildlife experts. The money granted by the company will fund a second colony that will increase the chances of survival of the species. One of the vulnerabilities of the wombat as a species is its concentration in one place—a forest fire or other natural disaster could easily wipe it out. By securing a second colony, its chances of survival are much greater.

At the original colony, conservation measures include controlling threats and managing habitat, accurately monitoring wombats, studying their biology and the ecology of their environment, and developing effective captive techniques on other wombat species.

"Having only one population of the NH Wombats is basically like having all your eggs in one basket."
—The Wombat Foundation

Threat	7/10
Uniqueness	7/10
Human responsability	8/10
Hope	6/10
Symbolism	4/10
Average score	6.4/10

Patrick Bonneville: This is the most astonishing goat of all. Its stylish corkscrew twisted horns are spectacular, but its chances for survival are alarming. If only it could be left out of humanity's crazy wars and race for oil, the species would be fine.

The markhor is considered by many big game hunters as one of the greatest trophies of all because of its horns, which can measure 1.5 meters (60 in.) long. Listed as endangered on the IUCN Red List, with only 2,500 individuals left in the world, the species faces extinction within a few years if the current trend continues.

The markhor lives on the summits of Central Asian mountains in Pakistan, Afghanistan, India (Kashmir), Tajikistan, and Uzbekistan. It is the largest of goats and emits a goaty scent to match its size. Females live with their young in flocks of up to nine members, and males are mostly solitary. Both males and females sport the twisting horns, although those of males are larger.

Although hunting the markhor is illegal in all the countries in which it lives, the main threat to its existence remains poaching. Pakistani wildlife authorities offer three permits per year to hunt the great trophy, with some of the money going to conservation programs. Recently, a Norwegian hunter paid $US 81,200 for a hunting permit.

Right: The male's horns can grow up to 160 cm (64 inches) long.
Above: Markhor mother with her two young.

Civic unrest and ongoing war make it difficult to undertake conservation programs or even to monitor the goat's population, which has declined by 20 percent in two generations. The overall population trend is still decreasing. Small grassroots programs have tried to stabilize the population but regional instabilities make it very difficult to measure any conversation efforts.

Threat	8/10
Uniqueness	4/10
Human responsability	7.5/10
Hope	8/10
Symbolism	4.5/10
Average score	6.4/10

The Hawaiian duck is native to Hawaii, where it once roamed all but two islands. It is now only found on Kaua'i and Ni'ihau. A reintroduction program on the islands of O'ahu, Hawai'I, and Maui has led to a recent downgrading of the duck's status on the IUCN Red List. It is now considered endangered, with an estimated population of about 2,200 in the wild.

The Hawaiian duck lives in wetlands of all kinds and will feed on whatever it can find. Its population decline is due largely to the loss of eggs through predators such as rats, mongooses, dogs, cats, and other non-native species. As duck hunting became an important sport, the population declined further. There was also a deterioration of its habitat, as settlers altered wetlands for agriculture or aquaculture plantations and introduced non-native plant life. In a further step to moderate the environment of the duck and other native species, the state of Hawaii enforces a rigorous ban on all imported birds to the islands.

"Few people today can say they've seen a Koloa maoli (Hawaiian duck), a petite and secretive bird and yet another of Hawaii's animals on the endangered species list."
—The Mālama Hawai'i Organization

Threat	8/10
Uniqueness	5/10
Human responsability	7.5/10
Hope	6/10
Symbolism	5/10
Average score	6.3/10

Left: Young Hawaiian ducks are born excellent swimmers. Soon after hatching, they take to the water, but they can only fly nine weeks later.
Above: Road sign in Haleakala National Park, Maui, Hawaii.
Right: The native Hawaiian name for this duck is *koloa maoli*.

The largest of all hammerhead sharks, this species has been placed in jeopardy by fishing nets. It prefers the tropical waters of the Gulf of Mexico, Caribbean Sea, Mediterranean Sea, and those of the Atlantic off the northern coast of Africa. The IUCN Red List evaluates the great hammerhead as endangered, as its population is estimated to have dropped by 80 percent in the past twenty-five years. It is considered critically endangered in the eastern Atlantic and in the Gulf of Mexico.

Hammerhead sharks are solitary creatures, which makes observation difficult. It is known that they are nomadic, migrate seasonally and are adaptable to their environment—they can live close to shore as well as in deep water. With a flexible diet that ranges from fish to crustaceans and cephalopods, it is able to feed in waters around the globe.

The great hammerhead is hunted for its fins, a main ingredient in shark fin soup, and is also killed as accidental bycatch in commercial fishing. Because bycatch statistics do not specify the genus of hammerhead shark caught in nets, there is some difficulty in gathering precise data related to this species' population decline. Since the great hammerhead prefers temperate oceans, it can be concluded that the sharks are victim to mass fishing techniques practiced there including fixed bottom nets, hook and line, and bottom trawls. Until 1986, Taiwan operated a great hammerhead fishery that targeted the sharks

throughout their ranges from Australia to China. Other fisheries have also been identified in Brazil, the eastern United States, and Mexico. Some sources show the hammerhead is worth about $US 50 per pound—with an average hammerhead weighing as much as 500 pounds (227 kg), the desire that drives the hunt is strong. Since these sharks reproduce only every two years, their population is unable to catch up.

There are no known active conservation measures in place for the great hammerhead, although it is listed in Annex I, *Highly Migratory Species*, of the UN Convention on the Law of the Sea. This document recommends cooperation throughout the shark's territorial ranges for the management of the population, however no state has yet expressed a desire to lead this project. A lack of adequate data and continuous monitoring add to the difficulty of such a management program.

Some promising actions have been taken by certain countries, such as the USA, the European Union, and Australia, who have banned "shark finning," or the removal of fins without any further use of the carcass. These plans need to be examined, improved, and implemented worldwide if the great hammerhead is to be saved.

Left: A 400-lb male hammerhead shark freshly fished. The hammerhead shark is an expensive delicacy, appreciated by many.

Threat	7/10
Uniqueness	6/10
Human responsability	7/10
Hope	6.5/10
Symbolism	5/10
Average score	6.3/10

There are two subspecies of this small prosimian: the red and the grey loris. While the grey is thriving in India and Sri Lanka, the total wild population of red loris is composed of fewer than 2,500 mature individuals, with no subpopulation containing more than 250. The population has declined steadily during the past decade, causing it to be upgraded from vulnerable to endangered on the IUCN Red List.

Red slender lorises are endemic to central and south-western Sri Lanka, where they prefer the treed canopies and dense vegetation of rainy coastal wet zones and rainforests. They will not live in human settlements. Red slender lorises grow to about 250 mm (seven inches) long and weigh no more than about 370 grams (thirteen ounces). They eat small animals, insects, and reptiles.

Lower left: The last remainig wild slender lorises live in the undisturbed forest of India and Sri Lanka.
Above: The species is no longer than 25 cm (10 in.) long.

Sri Lanka has seen this primate's population decrease by more than 80 percent over the past 200 years; a further decline of 10 percent is expected within the next two to three years. Loss of habitat, road kill, and hunting for both the pet trade and traditional medicine industries are major threats. Some studies show that loris can be electrocuted by power lines and some are subject to superstition killings. Currently, the loris is listed on CITES Appendix II and is also protected under the Fauna and Flora Protection Ordinance Act No. 2 of 1937, as well as its subsequent amendments. To further protect the red slender loris, research and management of the remaining populations must be implemented.

Threat	7/10
Uniqueness	7.5/10
Human responsability	6/10
Hope	5/10
Symbolism	6/10
Average score	6.3/10

Despite its name, the Cuban crocodile was once found throughout the Caribbean. It is now found only in Cuba's Zapata swamp and on Isla de Juventud. It is listed as critically endangered by the IUCN, as its population has declined by more than 80 percent. There are about 4,000 Cuban crocodiles left in the wild today.

This crocodile is considered highly intelligent and is at home in both ground and water ranges. They have been observed hunting in packs and have strong jaws with up to sixty-eight large teeth that can easily crush a turtle shell. They can be up to 3.5 meters (11 ft.) long and can live for up to seventy-five years.

Cuban crocodiles are threatened by habitat loss, hybridization with native American crocodiles, and illegal hunting for meat for the tourism industry. Their eggs are an easy food source for other animals as well as for young crocodiles.

In the 1950s and '60s, farms were set up to breed the Cuban crocodile for meat and skin; during this time, they were extensively cross-bred with the American crocodile. Since then, a pure-race group has been located and efforts are being made to prevent further cross-breeding. Other direct measures that will help this crocodile survive are captive breeding programs, reintroduction to the wild, and the creation of protected regions.

*"The restricted area occupied by Cuban crocodiles needs to be given effective protection to ensure the survival of the species in the wild."
—IUCN-SSC Crocodile Specialist Group*

Threat	8/10
Uniqueness	5/10
Human responsability	6/10
Hope	6/10
Symbolism	6/10
Average score	6.2/10

Left: The Cuban crocodile lives mainly in swamps and calm rivers.

Patrick Bonneville: Its cousins, the western long-beaked echidna and Sir David's long-beaked echidna, are also critically endangered.

The eastern long-beaked echidna is a spiny animal of the monotreme order, which is made up of mammals that lay eggs rather than give birth to live offspring. The platypus is the only other such mammal. Also known as Barton's long-beaked echidna, this small animal lives in New Guinea, where more than 80 percent of its population has disappeared over the last forty-five to fifty years. The IUCN Red List considers it critically endangered.

Now extinct in Papua New Guinea, its distribution has grown sparse in its other traditional ranges in the central mountains of New Guinea and Indonesia, and in the Foja Mountains of Indonesia. Historically, the echidna was commonly found from sea level to around 4,150 meters (13,500 feet); today, however, it is next to impossible to find any at sea level.

The smallest of the echidnas, the eastern long-beaked echidna rolls into a small ball for defense and uses its quills for protective armor. It also has spiny tongues that help it catch the worms and insect larvae that make up its diet. After laying an egg, a female deposits it in her pouch, where it hatches after ten days. The baby, called a puggle, remains there for up to fifty-five days.

The long-beaked echidna was hunted for food to the point of extinction in the more populated and accessible regions of its territories. The last confirmed sighting of the species was in the Cyclops Mountains in 1961. Its habitat has become compromised by deforestation, mining, and human encroachment, and, unfortunately, tits spread-out population means that conservation is difficult to monitor.

Above: When attacked, the eastern long-beaked echidna rolls into a spiny ball to defend itself.
Right: The animal weighs from 5 to 10 kg (11–22 lb).

Threat	7/10
Uniqueness	7/10
Human responsability	7/10
Hope	6/10
Symbolism	4/10
Average score	6.2/10

Left: Slightly smaller than a domestic cat, the island fox l is 48–50 cm (18–20 in.)long, excluding its tail, and the animal weighs between 1.3 and 2.8 kg (2.8–6.2 lbs.).
Right: Panorama of the California mainland from Channel Islands National Park, the natural habitat of the island fox.

This unique fox lives on six of southern California's eight Channel Islands. Each of the six subspecies is unique to the island it lives on. It is listed as critically endangered by the IUCN. In 2002, the total population was estimated at 1,500 foxes on all the islands.

The island fox is smaller than the grey fox and smaller than an average-sized domestic house cat. Predation by the Golden eagle, food supply, and habitat loss are the main reasons for its scarcity. Non-native animals—including cats, pigs, sheep, and goats, as well as American bison—also play a role in the fox's decline. An interesting example of the evolution of the practice of conservation is that previously, island foxes were euthanized in order to conserve an island bird species called the loggerhead shrike. Foxes were raiding the nests at breeding time. Now, however, foxes are held in captivity until the bird breeding season ends, and they are then released back into their territories.

Remaining fox populations throughout the Channel Islands are under intense observation. While there are some captive breeding programs, there is concern that these individuals will not be able to survive in the wild without having learned how to avoid the Golden eagle from their parents. Nevertheless, conservationists hope that re-introduced foxes will boost the overall population enough to allow eventual reproduction and stabilization without further human intervention. In 2009, the Santa Cruz Island fox population had increased from fewer than 100 to about 700—a very positive step for the species.

"The fossil record shows evidence of foxes on Santa Rosa Island dating back 10,400 to 16,000 years ago."
—American National Park Service

Threat	8/10
Uniqueness	5/10
Human responsability	7/10
Hope	6/10
Symbolism	4/10
Average score	6.2/10

Kim Murray: An endangered pigeon? This is surely a sign that humans need to catch up fast with species conservation!

The rare Marquesan imperial pigeon is endemic to remote regions of Nuku Hiva in the Marquesas Islands, French Polynesia. There are about 170 birds in the wild, although recent research indicates there may be about 30 more birds than earlier believed. Listed as critically endangered only a few short years ago, in 2008 the IUCN downgraded this bird to endangered because of the successful establishment of a second population.

Above: One of the rare photos of a wild Marquesan imperial-pigeon. It lives in remote areas freed of humans and predators .

Although hunting is illegal and education campaigns have been effective, poaching still remains a concern. Habitat loss has also been a threat, as territory was converted for cattle grazing. Cattle are no present in the bird's territory, and pig and goat populations are decreasing. Rats and cats continue to pose a danger, however, as they actively hunt and kill the pigeon. Future conservation efforts should include measures to design vehicle roads that take into account the bird's well-being. Since the Marquesan imperial pigeon bird is endowed with a great level of respect by local culture, saving it is vital.

"The occurence of this species in only one island makes its situation extremely fragile."
—The Ornithological Society of Polynesia - "MANU"

"Unfortunately, this biodiversity has been exposed to almost two millennia of human disturbance. Several species have gone extinct in known history and much of the flora and fauna is critically endangered."
—The World Wildlife Fund about the tropical Marquesas Islands

Threat	8/10
Uniqueness	6/10
Human responsability	6/10
Hope	7.5/10
Symbolism	3/10
Average score	6.1/10

Known as the Kakī in Māori, this shorebird is native to New Zealand. Despite twenty years of intensive conservation efforts, this species remains one of the most threatened in the world; there are only about forty-two black stilts in the wild and some sixty in captivity. They are listed as critically endangered by the IUCN.

The long-legged wading birds have black feathers and are about forty centimeters (16 inches) long. They wander near the shores of rivers looking for the insects and, the small fish they occasionally eat. They are mostly sedentary, with only a small portion of the South Island population flying to the North Island for the winter.

They were once numerous throughout both the North and the South Islands, however in 1981 only twenty-three birds remained. Non-native species introduced to the islands constituted the bird's main threat, especially cats, ferrets, and rats, who destroy nests as they search out eggs. The black stilt's natural environment is particularly vulnerable to changes caused by hydro-electric projects.

Intensive conservation programs since the late 1980s have included captive breeding and predator control. The captivity center at Twizel engages in a practice known as "double clutching," or removing eggs from the nest so the parents will lay more. The center then cares for the young birds and raises them, and reintroduction efforts are estimated to have an 80-100 percent success rate. Double-clutching eggs in the wild is also practiced. Conservation efforts seem to be working, and as of 2006, seventeen breeding pairs were recorded. These projects have saved the bird from extinction, but long-term survival will depend on the continued efforts of the various programs.

Threat	7/10
Uniqueness	5.5/10
Human responsability	7/10
Hope	5.5/10
Symbolism	5/10
Average score	6.0/10

The whooping crane is native to all of North America but is now extinct in Mexico. It is listed as an endangered species on the IUCN Red List because of its small population that has little natural growth in the wild.

Before the European settlement of North America, the whooping crane was once a thriving species with thousands of adults throughout the continent. The only natural wild population today breeds in Wood Buffalo Natural Park in northern Alberta, Canada and winters near the Aransas National Wildlife Refuge, in Texas, USA.

By 1938, there were a mere fifteen adults left. Over-hunting and human disturbances were the major cause of decline, however, today the greatest danger it faces is collision with power lines. Management and conservation of the natural wild population as well as establishment of reintroduced populations are helping to improve genetic health and increase breeding. The birds are being reintroduced to the wild in natural parks and reserves where they are protected, and efforts to raise the public's awareness about the vulnerability of the whooping crane also show promise. There is evidence that the population is increasing: in December 2007, there were an estimated 382 birds counted from a total of three different wild populations, two of which were created from reintroduction programs.

"For the Whooping crane there is no freedom but that of unbounded wilderness, no life except its own."
—Researcher Robert Porter Allen

WILDLIFE CONSERVATION

WHOOPING CRANES

U.S. POSTAGE 3¢

OF ISSUE

Threat	7/10
Uniqueness	5.5/10
Human responsability	6/10
Hope	5/10
Symbolism	5.5/10
Average score	5.8/10

Opposite page: Whooping crane with a blue crab in the Aransas National Wildlife Refuge, Texas.
Left: In 1957, the whooping crane was featured on a U.S. postage stamp supporting wildlife conservation.

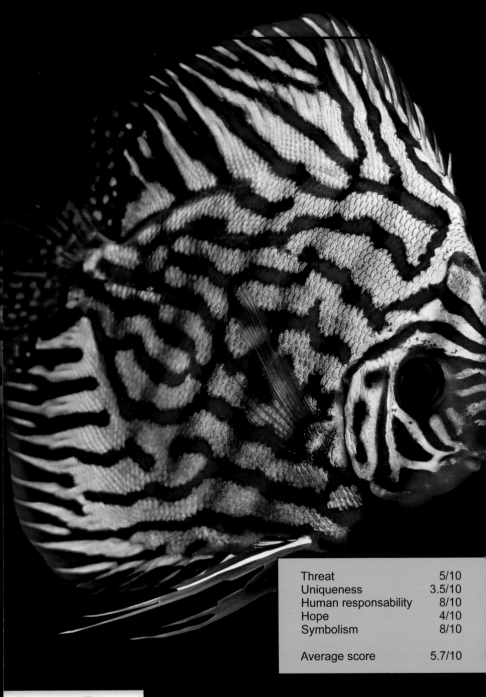

Threat	5/10
Uniqueness	3.5/10
Human responsability	8/10
Hope	4/10
Symbolism	8/10
Average score	5.7/10

Cichlids are small fish from the large and diverse Cichlidae family, in which there are at least 1,300 different identified species. New species are discovered regularly, making this one of the largest vertebrate families on earth. This in itself makes it very difficult to protect the specific sub-species that are in danger of extinction.

Cichlids are freshwater fish most commonly found in Africa and South America. Some subspecies are found in North America, Central America, Japan, and Australia. According to the IUCN Red List, there are currently 156 species listed as vulnerable, 40 as endangered, and 69 as critically endangered. At least forty-five species are now extinct—thirty-nine of them within the last two decades.

Threats to the species include non-native fish introduction, deforestation—which causes water quality degradation—and overfishing. Some species are bottom dwellers and are affected by bottom-trawling fishing, which destroys the lake floor and depletes food stocks.

A perfect example of the extreme delicate balance of this species can be found in Lake Malawi, Africa, home to the highest variety of cichlids worldwide. Of the 640 known varieties, over 600 are endemic to this lake. Many are on the verge of extinction mostly because of the introduction of the Nile Perch, which was introduced as a food source for humans. Cichlids generally have few bones and a pleasant taste and are therefore fished for human consumption.

Some species are considered exotic and demand a high price tag, and others are hunted for sport, such as the peacock bass of South America. Some cichlids are small and make excellent aquarium fish. Such fish can easily be farmed and consequently it is believed that the aquarium industry, for the moment, has little impact on the wild populations. More research and data are needed to properly evaluate that risk. Some believe that aquarium culture is beneficial to the cichlid, since collecting the fish in the wild has the side effect of promoting and protecting the reefs where they are found.

Conservation efforts vary, but in general, cichlids do not generate sympathy and few programs appear to be in place. Some African regions do offer support for cichlid protection, but efforts are poorly organized and widely dispersed.

Left: Since the 1940's, cichlids have become very popular as aquarium fish, bringing color to our world.
Right: There are at least 1,300 scientifically described species of cichlids, with a wide variety of colors and sizes.

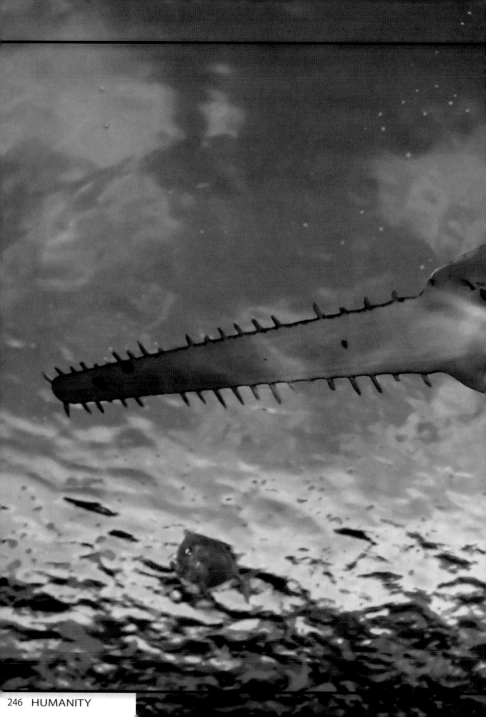

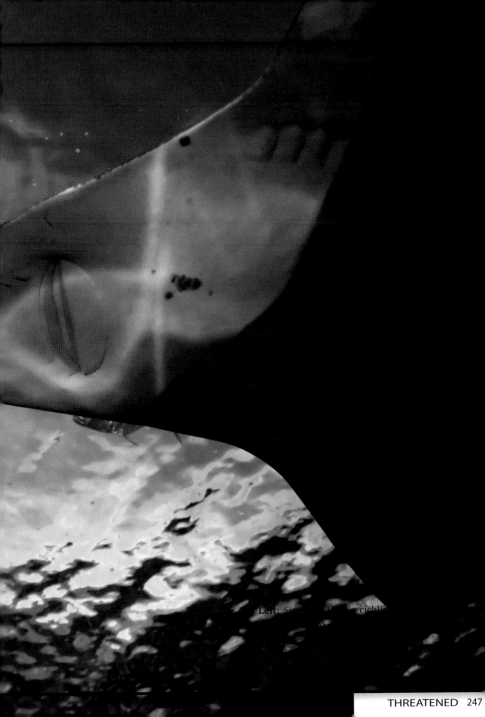

Left: S... ...cichli...

Patrick Bonneville: Our last threatened species, but not the least. When I saw the sawfish listed on the IUCN Red List, I knew we had to put it the book. The loss of this fish would be a loss for humanity. How do you go about saving a species that lives in oceans? I'm not convinced that humans, even with plenty of goodwill, can turn around such a trend. It looks like the end for the sawfish.

There are seven species of sawfish in the world. According to IUCN experts, they are all critically endangered. Although it superficially resembles a shark, the sawfish is actually a member of the ray family of fish. Its distinctive long, toothy snout, called a rostrum, is a sensing tool that is used to detect the movement and heartbeats of its prey. The fish waves its nose back and forth over the sandy ocean bottom, much like a security guard's wand at the airport security check. The rostrum is also used as a digging tool.

Sawfish are found in tropical and sub-tropical regions of the Atlantic and Pacific oceans. The wide sawfish is also present in the Gulf of Mexico. Some species once lived in the Mediterranean Sea and others are now becoming very rare on the African Atlantic coast. All the species are able to adapt to both freshwater and saltwater.

The major threat to the sawfish's survival is targeted and bycatch fishing. It is often caught in nets and lines set for other species, since its long "saw" easily gets stuck in any sort of net gear—the Western African population of sawfish has been especially affected by fishing activities. It is also valued for their meat and its rostrum is prized on the black market. Its slow rate of reproduction means that overfishing claims more of the population than can be replenished.

Various countries whose waters are in the sawfish's range have banned targeted fishing and the trade of sawfish parts, except for conservation purposes. Perhaps because of its increased rarity, there is an increasing demand for live sawfish for public aquariums, where it has great value as a commercial attraction. These "genetic lifeboats" will at least serve to preserve some of the species, however long-term measures to save the sawfish must include protected waters where fishing nets may not be placed.

"Scientists have concluded that this sawfish population has declined by as much as 99 percent and is in danger of extinction."
—*Ocean Conservancy*

Threat	3/10
Uniqueness	9/10
Human responsability	6/10
Hope	4/10
Symbolism	3/10
Average score	5.7/10

Left: The sawfish can reach 7 m (23 ft) in length.

PHOTO CREDITS

PHOTO CREDITS

203	Reinhold68/Dreamstime.com
204 l	Joanne Harris&Daniel Bubnich/Shutterstock
204 b	Eric Isselée/Shutterstock
204 r	Kirk Peart Imaging/Shutterstock
205	Dave Pape
205 b	Michael Schmeling/Dreamstime.com
206	Anothergecko/Dreamstime.com
206	sergge/Dreamstime.com
207	Chestert/Dreamstime.com
208	Kevin McKereghan
208 b	Michael Schmeling/Dreamstime.com
209	Terrance Emerson/Dreamstime.com
210	Kjersti Joergensen/Dreamstime.com
212	Kjersti Joergensen/Dreamstime.com
213 b	Kjersti Joergensen/Dreamstime.com
213	Csaba Vanyi/Dreamstime.com
214	Vyacheslav Markovnin/Dreamstime.com
215	Shargaljut/Dreamstime.com
216	Jorge Luis Brocca
217	Lucas Bluff
217 b	Sunflowerhike/Dreamstime.com
218 r	American Bureau of Land Management
218 b	teamosa - Sharon
218 l	Coz
219	Jiri Castka/Dreamstime.com
220	Perception/Dreamstime.com
220 b	Serban Bogdan/Dreamstime.com
221	Robert Paul Van Beets/Dreamstime.com
222	Greksa/Dreamstime.com
224	Photohomepage/Dreamstime.com
225	Sonya Etchison/Dreamstime.com
226	Paparico/Dreamstime.com
226 r	Ron Chapple Studios/Dreamstime.com
227	Paparico/Dreamstime.com
228	John Stublar/Dreamstime.com
230 b	Kathy Wynn/Dreamstime.com
231	truebeast
232 r	Alpana Bhartia, People For Animals
232 l	Andrey Melkozyorov/Dreamstime.com
232 b	Joao Virissimo/Dreamstime.com
233	Amwu/Dreamstime.com

234	Sylvie Lebchek/Dreamstime.com
234 b	Jiri Moucka/Dreamstime.com
235	Rossco/Dreamstime.com
236 b	Shelly Greer/Dreamstime.com
236	National Park Service
237	Jay Beiler/Dreamstime.com
238	Ivonne Wierink/Dreamstime.com
239	Yang Zhang
239	Dmitryp/Dreamstime.com
239 b	Darknightsky/Dreamstime.com
240	Norman Bateman/Dreamstime.com
242	Paul Wolf/Dreamstime.com
243 b	Brian Dunne/Dreamstime.com
243	John Kropewnicki/Dreamstime.com
244	Moori/Dreamstime.com
245	Wawritto/Dreamstime.com
246	Ryhor Zasinets/Dreamstime.com
247	Alejandro Castillo/Dreamstime.com
247 b	Rcaucino/Dreamstime.com
248	Artbyallyson/Dreamstime.com
254	Chris Lorenz/Dreamstime.com
256	Ekaterina Solovieva/Dreamstime.com